언니. Unni.
Older Sister.

Older Sister.
Not Necessarily Related.

JENNY HEIJUN WILLS

McClelland & Stewart

Library and Archives Canada Cataloguing in Publication data is available upon request

ISBN: 978-0-7710-7089-1
ebook ISBN: 978-0-7710-7090-7

Typeset in Jenson Pro by M&S, Toronto
Printed and bound in Canada

McClelland & Stewart,
a division of Penguin Random House Canada Limited,
a Penguin Random House Company

www.penguinrandomhouse.ca

1 2 3 4 5   23 22 21 20 19

Penguin
Random
House

For C. Take my hand.

Preface

This story, these stories are not all mine. Some of them, in fact, belong to no one at all, but are the fantasies that seem to flower so naturally from the mouths of those of us who've grown lives out of half facts, wishful thinking, and outright lies. Who piece themselves together from the residue of lost records. From withheld or secreted records. Whose orphanages and agencies have been evasively destroyed by fire and flood. Or by shame. We are told there's nothing left of the people or places or lives we might have had. We're told they—and our knowledge of them—do not belong to us. They never did. And so, these stories are nothing special—only echoes of memories and alibis. But they are all I have.

I.

가지. Gah-jee.

Branch.

⸭<

Minutes after I was born, my grandfather—that is, my father's father—gifted me a name. Then he signed a contract that struck me from the family registry. That ripped me away from my mother as she frantically counted my wrinkled and already-reaching fingers and toes. She pressed her mouth to my wet hair only once before I was taken away, what remained of the salty wax slip of her own insides thick and earthy on her lips.

For thirty years (and still to this day in the mouths of most), my name was replaced by one so expected it might have been Jessica or Meghan or Kimberly. Names of varying degrees of impossibility to Korean speakers. Mine is a name that I answer to, but that I wear only because I'm accustomed to it. Because others are accustomed to it. Not because it suits me. Early on, I was scrubbed until my skin turned pink. I was programmed to speak English, then French, and to place my fork and knife side by side on my plate when I had finished eating. I disappeared into a life of cream-of-mushroom casseroles, Irish setters, and patent leather Sunday school shoes. I was buried under Bach concertos, feathered bangs, and maple sugar candy until my own mother wouldn't have recognized me.

But of course I couldn't stay missing forever, and around 2009, I was reborn somewhere in the dusky November mountains of Seoul. I came back to life with a long wooden spoon in one hand and flat silver chopsticks in the other. I came back when my Korean father called me by name, when my Korean mother called me daughter. When my youngest sister called me unni, older sister, and I understood what that meant.

I learned by mimicking others. I tried to fall in line with a culture practised by people who use given names only for those younger than themselves. I peeled giant apples in one long curl. I recognized spiciness by the redness in the bowl. I came back to life when all the ginkgo berries had fallen and the entire country of South Korea was filled with their cutting scent. I came back to life when all that remained were persimmons clinging to bare branches.

While my homecoming was something to be celebrated, it also planted lingering heartache once all the soju had been drunk and all the kisses had been given and received. I watched my parents, reunited after being torn apart on the day I was taken, fumble through what could have been our lives, if only. They came together, reclaimed the love they'd lost decades earlier. They thought they'd outsmarted fate. I thought I was happy.

I watched my own unni's life crack and splinter and shatter when it became clear that our father had always been pathetic and her mother had sometimes been both weak and cruel. She tried, my unni, to love me despite all the disloyalty that went into my making, but in the end we had nothing to hold on to. And although there is even less between us now, I still whisper stories to her into the sky, fallen eyelashes and dandelion fluff. Confessions and prayers to an older sister, related but not really. Wishes that, one day, everything will be forgiven.

Not actually a tree but a wooden vine that reaches skyward and pulls itself up, wisteria unfurls its fingers to the forest floor, beautiful strangler. Where do I fall on this insistent branch that erupts in tangles, shaking its loveliness in the wind as it chokes its neighbours and itself? A stem where two other branches meet? My father's branch was already heavy with the weight of an older brother and sister. My mother's would blossom another brother and sister not long after I was lopped off. How gorgeous it all is until one draws back the locks of flowers and finds the poisonous seeds at its core.

When I was growing up, schoolyard rumour had it that my Korean mother was a sex worker and my Korean father was a fisherman. And that my mother was poor and my father was married. And that I had two older brothers, on my father's side. That's why, the mostly untrue gossip suggested, they decided to send me away. At home, there was also a story going around that I had been cared for by a foster family who fed me applesauce and rice pudding. That was unconfirmed, but what is known is that by the time I first arrived in Canada as a nine-month-old infant in the early 1980s, someone had already taught me how to say *ummah*, meaning mommy, and because it was my first and only word, I repeated it over and over again, entertaining my new family, who made note but decided it was meaningless baby babble. Decades later, when I was grown, I felt as if I was sailing away the exact moment I realized the cruelty of having learned that word at all. Anyhow, it was reported that as a baby I slept on my stomach. It was a well-known fact that no one paid a dime for me—that is, except for agency fees, taxes, day-to-day upkeep, airline tickets, and other incidentals. This bears repeating. The costs were high, but it was not me per se that was so valuable. It was common knowledge that my new parents had considered Vietnam first, but it was closed to Canadians. They didn't care. They just wanted to help.

❀<

The way his hair was greying salt-and-pepper at his temples. How his thick eyebrows arched when he laughed, the black-blue patina of a crow's wing. I watched him closely out of the corner of my eye. I didn't speak. He was different from all the others in the group. He sat cross-legged, like me, so our knees sometimes touched underneath the low table with the sunken centre where meat was being grilled. I'd never seen a table like that or a man like him ever before. It was 2008 and I was twenty-seven. He was older. I overheard him talking to someone else about his child. A daughter.

That night in Chicago we drank the way those who'd been back had witnessed Koreans drinking. Large bottles filled small glasses with unremarkable beer, but still we ordered and paid and ordered some more, knowing the import fees were inflated. The man next to me moved confidently as he splayed marinated meat on the grill. It curled at the edges. I imagined it still alive, retreating into itself in sadness. He spread fermented soy paste onto lettuce leaves as though he'd been doing it his entire life. I watched but didn't follow. I might have wrongly guessed he was Korean-Korean. Or Korean American, grown in a family of people who looked and acted and ate like him. But really, he was like the rest of us, who'd arrived in the Midwest for a conference and found ourselves disconnected again, this time from racial kin who'd not been raised in white homes and communities as we'd been. Asian American scholars whose knowledges of their racial selves hadn't needed to be self-taught in adulthood. Probably alone. Possibly in secret. But we were, at that table, siblings in our ongoing and always changing dislocations.

There were many of us that night in the smoky Korean barbecue restaurant. As a child, I knew of one other person like me, and maybe we'd seen each other as toddlers, but there'd never been a connection. That night at that table in a suburb of Chicago, we were about twenty. Without even trying, without knowing it, those people changed my life forever. I saw them through the smoke that turned our eyes red. And they saw me.

Many years later, in a hotel room in California, I leaned into that man and let him hold on to me for a moment. He'd become even more handsome over time and by then I knew how to eat Korean food and sit at a Korean table. We never fell in love. But I recognize that on that Chicago night the quiet desire I felt for him was the start of something unspeakable.

I don't remember what I said in that introduction, but I'm sure it was out of character. I like to keep parts of my heart buried deep. I've learned to hold myself hard and intact. But those adoption agencies, they feed on sentiment, get off on the spectacle of reunion, even though they are perpetrators of our conditions in the first place. Maybe *perpetrators* isn't the right word. How about *profiteers*? Anyhow, if and when we decide to search, they make us fill out a form with what we think is our name, our parents' names, our birthdate. We put all our faith in those make-believe things and hand ourselves over because we have no other choice.

A social worker in the post-adoption services unit told me she'd located my mother only one week after I'd reached out to their offices. I asked for the contact information but was refused. She, at once the person who held the few pebbles of my Korean life in her hand and the person who closed her fingers into a fist around them, insisted I write a letter to Ummah, to be translated and delivered by the agency, if I wanted to gain access.

And so I wrote from a place of humiliation, where the words *Dear Mother* sat alone on the computer screen for hours, my heart beating in time with the blinking cursor, or maybe it was the other way around. I didn't know how to begin. Or what to call her. I didn't know what to say to make her love me. Or at least want me. Maybe if I'd been younger, say in my early instead of late twenties, it would have felt more natural. It might have been easier, finding that balance between modesty and boastfulness, self-effacement and seduction. But by the time I wrote that letter, I was deep into my studies, exploring the stories we tell about our adopted selves and that are told about us. I knew, all too well, how uncertain the process of coming back together can be. Although I was living alone in Cambridge for the year, all of a sudden I was crowded by questions of how I might continue moving forward when my past wasn't yet dealt with. I was afraid to misstep. To overwhelm her with my desire. I was afraid, once again, to be unwanted.

I knew how important that letter was, but when it came time to write, I had nothing.

Unni . . . Maybe you won't believe me, but not once did I let myself picture her, my mother, from the time I was a little girl up until the moment I saw her at last. When I did see that photograph, though . . . Have you ever touched something so hot that it felt like ice? Have you ever fallen in love so fast you thought you might die?

Before that time, I never dared dream that I would meet her. I'd been conditioned to accept its impossibility. Cautioned by well-intentioned non-adoptees and non-Koreans that the cultural gap was too broad to overcome. Warned about how our mothers move on with their lives. How they didn't want us back then and that time only hardens them. Even chided that it is selfish to interrupt our mothers when we have perfectly fine lives in our adopted families and lands. That we are best kept as secrets, forever illegitimate and hidden.

And then, how Korean society has changed but not enough to forgive mothers who sent their children away. Who, in the first place, became those kinds of mothers in the ways that they did. Yet the same people who uttered those particular cautions, the other Korean adoptees I met because my studies took me out of the remoteness of Canada and into the U.S., where most of us end up, also admitted that even as they knew the odds were against them, they couldn't help searching either. That it was probably futile but still, they tried. And although I insisted I was ambivalent about finding her, and I guess by extension any of you, one night, in that ground-floor apartment near Harvard Square, I filled out reunion forms, sent them to my agency in Seoul, and prayed to be an exception.

In the end, I wish there'd been something more selfless, more spiritual even, that propelled me towards Korea and all of you. Ghosts haunting peripheries, their tangles of black hair twisting always just out of reach. Another pair of black eyes peering back not from a mirror but from a live person, the familiar curve of similar eyelids blinking. An abdominal twitch, a tightening, at the unreasonable goal of finding my mother before even considering motherhood myself. Even the practical and protective desire to graft a branch of my own onto some kind of medical-history family tree. None of these was the reason I looked.

It was fear.

Fear that I'd die, or that she would, before we could confess ourselves to one another. What did we have to confess? Well, in the first place, unni, she had to tell me why she did the things she did. But I also needed to explain myself and the anger and sadness that I couldn't release. That her loss, our loss, hadn't necessarily been in my best interests after all. At least not in the tidy way most people would like to believe. That maybe I had wasted the gift that she, that everyone, had thought I'd been given. And maybe I didn't see it as a gift at all.

For exactly nine months I sent emails to that agency in Seoul, which were then converted from English to Korean, printed, and mailed the old-fashioned way to a mother I eventually became comfortable calling by that title. Her initial letter, the response to my translated introduction, opened with my name and closed with it too. She wrote, *Heijun!* With an exclamation mark. When my eyes, which had been skimming the message as one's eyes do when they're nervously scanning for signs of rejection, fell upon my name sung out like that, they filled immediately.

I tried it on, that name I'd always hesitated to claim as my own in case I mispronounced it.

I may have misunderstood something she tried to explain later, but I think it was from the agency worker that my mother first learned my name in 2008. My Korean name. No one had told her what my grandfather called me in those surrender papers. What was printed in my first passport. No one told her what the daughter she never allowed herself to think about was named before that piece too was pushed out of the way. When we met face to face, my mother was careful to call me by my Canadian name. I assume that same agency worker guided her.

Ummah's letters appeared sporadically even though I replied always the same day hers were received. They were at once intimate and instructive, the way a mother's communication often is. She summarized my siblings in a few paragraphs. They could not, for many of the months we exchanged letters, know about me. And then all of a sudden they did, and I received a long message from a younger sister with a different father. At that time, I couldn't have known she would become the most important person in all of this. Seven years were between Bora and me, but more than that, language, culture, and the tragic beauty of discovering each other and then pondering what it meant that one of us had been kept and one sent away.

I planned my return for late summer 2009. My homecoming. Ummah was both impatient for me to arrive and uninterested in the travel arrangements. I applied for a research fellowship at a women's college in Seoul, taking advantage of one of the few connections I had over there. Later I learned Bora was a student at that very school. At times, when the weeks between letters from Korea became too many, I threatened to no one but myself that I would cancel everything. I came to understand after a while that my mother's boyfriend, a conservative man from her church, didn't approve of our reunion. He didn't approve of me. Or maybe it was that he wouldn't have approved so she never told him. I was always unclear on that. All I know is that she had to write in secret. She hinted at this in a hastily written letter sent only a few weeks before I was to return, and so I forgave her inconsistency and made plans to live in an adoptee guesthouse that cost roughly ten U.S. dollars a night.

4<

It was July and I was in Montreal shortly before leaving for Korea. I was staying in my boyfriend's apartment near Jean-Talon Market. It was like every Montreal summer—humid but with people swarming crowded markets, sidewalk sales, brunch spots. The energy of the city hummed white noise around me. I was already gone. In my heart I'd already left. But I'd not yet landed anywhere.

I didn't hear from my mother from the time I booked my flight until that short, apologetic explanation for her silence. For too long she'd fallen away from the agency, so the social workers could only apologize each time I asked. I felt a cloud wrapping itself around me, about to lift off with me inside. My Canadian parents visited Quebec around that time. They warned that in Korea the roads would be unpaved. That the food would be untrustworthy. *Dogs.* They said. *Those people eat dogs.*

In the middle of the night, only a few days before we were to leave, I shattered into a million pieces. Rain had finally come and the city exhaled in relief. I stood out on the street lit by the pulses of lightning edging closer by the minute, because that's what we did in those moments when the heat broke. My face was wet with rainwater, so I let myself cry unnoticed by anyone around me.

I cried because I was scared no one would be on the other side to pull me back down to the world. That maybe my mother wasn't really there. Or maybe she'd changed her mind. That I'd forever be reaching, offering my love

and myself to someone who didn't want it. Who still
didn't want me. While everyone else threw back their
heads, opened their mouths and arms to be washed over
and filled by the storm, I whispered to myself: *I'm still lost.*

We left the body of the airplane mostly in silence, my boyfriend and I. Only a few passengers muttered their appreciation to flight attendants whose black hair was starting to fall loose from wooden hair clips shaped a little like otgoreums tied at the front of hanboks. We stumbled out half-digested from the eighteen hours since our connection in Atlanta, squinting now because the blinds had been drawn down when the plane crossed the Arctic Circle's unblinking sunlight. So long had we been sitting in darkness. The walking pace immediately became Korean. We matched it, melting into and trusting the throng of people rushing in the direction of something they all recognized but we did not. Once past immigration, once through the wall separating the air-conditioned order of the airport from the strangled madness of the city beyond it, I hailed a taxi as if I was any other Korean woman in that place. I was home.

For four months, from late August until mid-December, I lived in that guesthouse for Korean adoptees who'd returned and were staying in Seoul. We ate and drank and slept together. Strangers at first, but then quickly not—the speed and force of our fast connections obvious ignition for the intensity of those relationships. The majority of the adoptees at the guesthouse were there for a month at most. The owners were kind and the volunteers worked hard. But it was a house of indulgence and discovery, and most times the revelry was too insistent. It was too deliberate. We tried to sanitize our wounds with alcohol, but our injuries are on the inside. Once, a young man who'd been raised in Norway was so drunk he fell down the winding staircase and stayed the rest of the night lying on the hard, unheated floor.

The guesthouse was more or less accessible by all the major subway lines. Tucked in from the road, it featured a rounded front section, glass doors, and a walkout basement. On one wall in the common living area, clocks were set to different time zones reflecting the locations where many of us had been raised. What was likely offered simply as a practical way to navigate the various and vast distances we'd travelled to come home was also a devastating reminder of how disconnected we all were. From each other, from Korea, and maybe also from our adoptive lands. If I remember correctly, most of the clocks were labelled after places like Norway and France.

I know for certain one clock indicated the time, specifically, in Minnesota. I'm not sure why I didn't look out the window the entire time I was there, but if I had, maybe the view would have been of sugar maples green at the moment of my arrival, red a few months in, and bare by the time I left.

For the first two weeks of my return, my boyfriend and I stayed on the top floor. We'd known each other for only a year and had spent much of our relationship on opposite sides of the Canada–U.S. border, so it hardly mattered that we were assigned separate rooms for sleeping; closeness across space was already familiar. I know I couldn't have made the trip to Korea without him. He held me up, held me together. He made it safe to come home, and by the time he left, I had a diamond ring on my left hand.

A few people, like me, stayed at the adoptee guesthouse while they went down the path of reuniting with family. Others were there to search. Many had simply succumbed to the pull of the country we'd all been torn from, were thrown out of, years earlier, and had no other place to live. I registered the grief of those looking for family when they had to share quarters with us fortunate ones who'd made contact. Many nights I sat with people from Germany, Denmark, the United States, Australia, listening to their sorrow and anger. Some applied for the chance to relay their information

on a Korean television program that reconnected
long-lost relatives, not just adoptees. I met one woman
who was featured on the show. Even after filming her
segment and giving over a blood sample to the producers,
she never did make contact. I also met a man who'd been
rejected by the program. A father himself, he'd left
behind his own child in Europe because he was so fixated
on finding the parents he'd lost decades earlier. He'd
been living, without documents, in Korea for a long time.
We cried together.

   That Seoul guesthouse was a place where adoptees
came to find kinship and support, where we tried to
assemble the shards of lives and a culture that were
tossed our way when we became too inconvenient to
unsee. But whatever it was that we made of those pieces
was indecipherable, so while the guesthouse was a place
where we forged the kinds of connections unavailable in
our regular lives, it was also a place of palpable confusion
and rage and grief. Someone once described it to me as a
space where Korean adoptee loss was concentrated.
Where one could witness how a decades-long program of
international adoption that began in 1953, one that
offered some benefits, could also spread devastation
across generations of people as it scattered hundreds of
thousands of us around the world. Where collateral
damages collided and drank themselves sick while
comparing notes on eerily similar childhoods of food

anxiety and abandonment issues that developed into adult eating disorders and abusive intimate partner relationships. Where we competitively offered to reveal our own scars if others showed us theirs first. Those people and their stories settled in my chest, calcified into a heavy mass that rattles in my heart when I think of my months in Seoul.

*Unni . . . It resonates a lot these days, that we who were
scraped up from the floor of orphanages and churches and
hospitals and sent alone to new families and cultures and
lands are members of a lost generation. We're a blip on the
history of your country, a nation that seems millennia older
than the countries to which we were sent. Our congregation
meets in adoptee guesthouses that are meant to keep us safe,
to give us hope even when the peoples and cultures we want
to dissolve into won't fully have us after all. When this ends—
and it will end, I promise you—a memorial will be built and
maybe pages will be added to grade-school textbooks. And
we'll continue to vanish, to die one by one, many of us with
the words why me? on our lips. I've heard official apologies
again and again, statements of remorse or shame that it is
still ongoing. But there is no true accountability if they keep
adding to our numbers. While they keep sending us so far
away. They're embarrassed this no-longer-necessary relief
program still exists. But, unni, it's just too good to give up.
Do you know how much people are still willing to pay?*

The day I again became an older sister has faded almost entirely from my memory. When I try to think back to that morning when my boyfriend—patient, worried, insistent—and I discovered the precision of the Seoul metro system, when we arrived an hour early at the modest offices of the Social Welfare Society, I'm aware that some details have fallen away. But I remember the weight of my mother's arms around me. I remember her yellow chiffon shirt and nervous smile. I remember my sister's silence. I deduced Ummah had taken an entire week off from work. Later, I wondered what she'd told her boss at the factory. What, if anything, she'd told her boyfriend at home.

It happened early morning the day after we landed in Korea.

The agency workers, they tried to choreograph the reunion. But it was unmanageable. Uncontrollable. I was too early, which foiled their plans, so they sent my boyfriend and me away for coffee, instructing us not to return for thirty minutes. I caught a glimpse of Ummah and Bora, recognizing them from their photographs, in an elevator as we were on our way to the café. Another social worker was frantically pushing the button to close the doors. The meeting had to happen as they'd planned, upstairs, when everyone was ready. When everyone was watching.

Later on, Bora would tell me how, in the moments leading up to the reunion, the agency worker spoke urgently to our mother and her about what they might expect from me when we finally met: sadness, confusion, and maybe even anger. Bora recounted the way Ummah braced herself each time footsteps could be heard in the hallway—holding her breath, curling her hands into fists, pressing her fingernails into her palms. And then the noise the door made when it swung open and the agency worker triumphantly stepped into the room and I was pushed forward.

I wasn't breathing.

Ummah rushed at me, her lost-then-found daughter. She threw her arms around me and held on. The situation was uncomfortable. I stopped myself from blinking, from moving my eyes at all, because I was embarrassed and afraid I might start crying. And everyone was watching. Ummah clung to me, but I didn't soften. Someone took my wrists in their hands and positioned my arms robotically around my mother so that, to an onlooker, we appeared to be embracing. I heard the artificial snap of a digital camera capturing the staged tableau. My jaw started to hurt because I was clenching it so tight. I was holding everything inside because I was ashamed by how much I was feeling. Over the years I'd learned how to harden my body around my emotions. To wait until it was safe to unfold.

The situation was devastating. It's mortifying to know someone so deeply but be meeting them for the first time. Ummah's hands were stroking my hair with the presumptuous intimacy a mother expects with her daughter. She moaned, over and over again, *I'm sorry*, in the language that had been ripped from my mouth before it had a chance to settle in. The agency worker offered me a tissue box, hinting that my lack of reaction was unappreciated. After all, so much planning had gone into this coming together. I ignored the tissues, but my boyfriend accepted some. He'd read all of the translated letters and listened to my fears leading up to the reunion, and his eyes were appropriately wet. Everyone was crying except me. I was just there.

Eventually, we took our seats on the couches that were set up around a melamine coffee table. Two more tissue boxes were lined up in perfect parallel there. Ummah sat next to me and held on to my hand as if I might sail away like a balloon if everyone was not careful. Her fingers entwined with mine and it felt as though I was holding a tiny bird in my fist. She was laughing in a way I'd later recognize was the discomfort of wanting to explain something important but not having the words to do it. Or the privacy. The agency worker gestured to Bora and made introductions. *You are Bora's unni*, she explained to me in English. *Her older sister. Her only sister.*

She was shy. My sister looked years younger than her actual age, which was twenty-one. When I presented the jewellery I'd brought as gifts, Ummah immediately adorned herself while Bora quietly bowed and slipped her present into her handbag. We barely spoke in that first meeting. But by the time I returned to the guesthouse that night, my sister had sent me an email, the contents of which are forever imprinted on my memory. It was the first time she called me unni. She said, *thank you for coming*. And when I saw her next, the tiny silver pendant was around her neck.

In a fitting room with only a draped curtain for privacy, I drew together my shoulder blades, making myself as narrow as possible, so that the thin fabric wouldn't tear when I slid the dress down onto me. It was raw silk. A shimmering taupe. Modest with its high collar and capped sleeves. Ummah and Bora had brought us to Insadong, a tourist quarter of Seoul. It was the morning after we'd first met. Together, we took the bus. I genuinely declined the dress, having not yet learned the dance of refusal that Koreans perform when offered a gift. The saleswoman insisted. I understood that she wanted the sale, but then she struck a place so deep inside that I recognized she knew something more than what she expressed. She held on to my wrist when, in English, she said what Ummah could not: *Mommy wants to buy her daughter a dress.*

Of course, I never once thought of myself as more than just a petal, a splinter, a feather plucked from the spectre of my mother's body. Even dreaming her into existence at the beginning of my search, from a faceless shadow into someone real, had taken all my courage, so I didn't dare think of the people whom she'd either confessed to or secreted me away from years ago. Maybe I wanted to envision her alone, with me heavy inside her, those nine months. Maybe I didn't have the imagination or the space to admit the family she had before me, who did or did not want me, who continued to be her people after I'd been sent away.

Back in Korea, I realized quickly how far the branches of my family stretched, how elaborate and tangled were its roots. I'd seen, in photographs shared before my arrival, a beautiful aunt. Imo was not much older than me. I'd also seen pictures of a younger brother, usurped when he was twenty-five of first-born status after the reappearance of an older sister he'd never known existed. But I'd not considered grandparents, uncles, cousins. Just as, to some of them, I seemed to materialize out of nothing, so too did they come into my consciousness without warning.

Ummah, I learned, had two older brothers. At least one, the eldest, knew of me. Maybe he even knew what happened when I was taken. He refused to see me when first I returned to Korea, and he died before my second trip back. His youngest daughter, though, offered a felt hair clip that I never wear but will hold on to always. Imo, my pretty aunt, had been told I'd died, and even as a child she'd known better than to ask how, or why, or when. My grandparents knew more of me than anyone else in the family. They wanted me back. Maybe they always had. And part of me wanted them too. Another part hated them and the way they carried on as family without me.

To meet my maternal grandparents, Bora, Ummah, my boyfriend, and I took the train from Seoul down to Gwangju, where imo was living at the time. Ummah had packed boiled sweet potatoes and corn, wrapped in aluminum foil, and we ate them plain but still warm while we raced past mountains and forests of ginkgo and cedar trees. Since the translator we'd hired was going to meet us there, we rode in silence. Melting in my luggage were the dragon's beard candies I'd bought on a second trip to Insadong, that time alone. A last-minute gift for elders I'd never thought of before. Strings of honey flossed around bundles of walnuts to make chalky, bite-sized pillows, instead of the more thoughtful presents I'd brought for the others: Gold and silver purchased at boulevard St-Laurent jewellery shops. A photo album that charted my life up until the age of seven, and then a gap, and then adulthood. On later trips to Korea, I followed the guidance of adoptee friends and packed multivitamins for my parents and grandparents. *To show them you care about their health,* they explained.

I met some of my extended family at my aunt's apartment, which was modern and white and had giant plastic flower wall decals. Imo's apartments, and by now I've seen a few of them, are always furnished in a Western style, with a dining table, beds, and sectional living room sets. We took a photo of the whole family sitting on a couch. My grandfather wore an expression on his face as though it was any other day. My grandmother's eyes were closed. I handed out my gifts and everyone marvelled, even at the sad last-resort candy. I was wearing the silk dress my mother had bought the week before. The translator, a young man who was probably a student, interpreted my grandfather's brief first words to me: *thank you for coming*. The same phrase my sister wrote the day we met. Halabuji watched me, amazed I'd found my way back. He said something else, something that took a long time, looking at me as if I understood. My eyes moved between him and the translator, hoping the younger man was listening. He wasn't, or he was uncomfortable recounting the words these strangers had expressed in front of him. Whatever the reason, I never learned what my grandfather said that day, those many minutes of confession or affection or chiding or something else. All I have is the memory of him trying to explain something to me, to help me make sense of the decades I'd been away.

⽊<

Part of me has always known that he proposed so that my Korean family would come back to me at least one more time. So that things wouldn't end at the beginning. Ummah'd promised, at the agency when we met, that she would travel to Canada for my marriage. He wanted to give that to me, and so, shortly after we arrived in Seoul, he asked and I said yes. In late August, lotus petals that had shed into the water floated on the surface of the pond at Changdeokgung Palace. The heady perfume that marks the end of life filled the garden. It started to rain and a mantis fell from a branch onto my shoulder. He had no ring and no plan. But he wanted to give me a future that he hoped would make up for my past.

Still, he had to leave one week later. And when he did, as I rode the metro from Incheon Airport back to Seoul by myself, the new weight of a ring purchased in the Jongno District awkward and heavy on my hand, I settled into a feeling I can only describe as hope-fear. I was afraid to be alone in a country that I wanted so much but that I could only ever really watch from afar. Yet also I was hopeful because, by myself, I would find out what I was made of.

It was mid-September when Ummah wanted to meet me at an outdoor café near the Myeong-dong station. I'd been in Korea for about a month, but we'd only met a handful of times. Her boyfriend, what little I knew of him, still disapproved. In the end, I'm unsure how much he knew about me at all. Maybe she understood him well enough to anticipate his upset, so she continued to keep me a secret even after I arrived. Or maybe she assumed that response after suffering for years with a husband who *did* know and weaponized the memory of me against her time and again. Perhaps it was easier to tell me that all these men disapproved than to admit she never acknowledged me in the first place. That she'd never found the courage to name me. Regardless, if Ummah wanted to see me during those months I was in Seoul, she had to start lies days in advance and pray that he would never find out.

In Seoul, I stood out in a crowd, so it wasn't difficult to spot me. Even though it'd been a month since my last salon visit, and my ash-blond hair was starting to show dark-brown roots, it was still a few years before that hair colour would become more commonplace in Korea. Thinking back, I wonder if I kept my hair light throughout that homecoming to mark myself as an outsider. Claiming difference for myself before any local Koreans could remind me that I did not quite belong.

I didn't notice my mother watching. I was looking at some cheap scarves laid out on a table. The worker eyed me distrustfully, maybe because I didn't respond when I was spoken to. Hooking my handbag over my shoulder, I selected two, a green one and a pink, and handed them to the cashier, who said something too quickly. From afar, Ummah registered the look of panic on my face. The worker, exasperated, held up all ten fingers and tried *arigato. Xie xie.*

Ummah hurried over and called out my Canadian name. I started laughing with my mouth open in the obvious way I always did. My head was thrown back. People were staring. Ummah spoke quickly in Korean, knowing I didn't understand. I put my hand on my hip and rattled off some disconnected Korean phrases before laughing again. The woman said something to Ummah, who hastily responded before leading me quickly away, holding my hand and not looking back.

Come here to me, I whispered low. My lips mouthed the words to no one at all, but to the unknowable country that defied any sense of logic. It was both so vast, so empty, and yet so tight and crowded at the same time. And every place that I witnessed for the first time was at once new and nostalgic. I willed it to enter me, angry that my request felt both desperate and pointless. I took some of those tours. The ones that start in a hotel lobby and stop at three or four different spots, with a rushed lunch served midday. The other tourists were mostly Japanese, but two young girls announced they were on school vacation from China. There also were a lot of Koreans. Koreans from Korea. There they were, paying for a guided tour of their own countryside, posing for photographs and climbing the steep mountain paths to see yet another carved Buddha.

Living in the adoptee guesthouse meant there were always people around. At times it was exhausting, so I'd leave—the risk of being alone in Seoul somehow worth it just for a moment of quietness. A chance to sit with myself and the weight of what was unfolding in my life. Once, on the metro, there was a young woman with a frizzed-out perm who was wearing too much makeup and had three holes in her wool leggings. She was half-sleeping. Worn out by whatever had happened the night before. Her head lolled from one side to the other, jerking upright every now and then when the brakes screamed or the train lurched around a bend. We were above ground suddenly, but she offered no acknowledgement. She captivated me. When she opened her eyes, she sneered at the other passengers, daring them to comment on the extra space she took up with her legs splayed wide apart. She sniffed audibly, this Korean woman who defied all the social rigours I'd been mimicking since I arrived. Pulling off her false-eyelash strips, starting at the inner corners, she flicked them onto the floor and snorted again.

It wasn't crowded at 11 a.m. on the green line. It was raining outside and I'd been riding the loop since before dawn. I knew some of the stops. Seoul National—where all the students disembarked. Ewha—where once I bought those flat boots I sensed would last a long time. Sillim—where Bora lived, though she'd never invited me to visit. I memorized the rhythm of the train when it breached at Hapjeong, an ocean beast cresting for air.

There was a soundtrack to the train. A few personal interest news stories, game shows, and advertisements —one for shampoo, another for liquor, both featuring sexy teenagers dancing—repeated at intervals of roughly seven minutes on the television monitors propped in the corners of the car. I liked the soju girls the best. On one of the game shows, participants were challenged to type songs on their cellphone keypads, the faster the better. It was before the time when smartphones would saturate the nation and then the world.

Two men, both about twenty, entered my train. I could tell by their accents they were American—from the Midwest. Minnesota, maybe. Or one of the Dakotas. They looked at me, evaluating me—but not in the way I'm used to. I heard them talking about me. They thought they'd found an easy one. Again, not in the way I'm used to. I knew then I was a double agent and I could see them coming a mile away. That day, in Seoul, I was camouflaged because I hadn't spoken or moved since boarding the metro. Approaching, they sat on either side of me even though there were many open spaces in the car. I didn't feel the usual fear that crept up when men cornered me like that. I channeled the frizzy girl's standoffish attitude, but failed. One of them held a Bible; the other, some pamphlets. They said something in

Korean that I didn't understand. I couldn't tell if they had passable accents. I didn't say anything, didn't reveal myself as a non-speaker. They gave up on me as I am sure they had on so many others. I was washed over by the thought that they saw me as any other Korean girl and not as a foreign outsider.

Eventually, the woman reached her stop. A nondescript station. I wondered if she was returning home from wherever her Saturday night had taken her. She deliberately kicked my shoe as she shuffled past, before waiting for the doors to open. I was probably staring. But it wasn't for the reasons she might have assumed. She impressed me because, in the quietness of a rainy Sunday morning, she didn't conform to what was wanted of her. She didn't care if she fit in, if other people rejected her—or at least she acted like someone who didn't care. I envied her. I pulled off my knit hat. A tangled mess of curly, dyed blond hair jutted out in all directions. My roots were an inch long. As she stepped onto the platform, I wondered if she noticed.

One night a group of adoptees came together in Myeong-dong or Hongdae or one of those places where we congregate. I was seated across from an adoptee who'd been raised in the U.S. and whose brazenness made me nervous. He bragged that his "American" accent was more valuable than any other, that he was able to charge more for private English tutoring lessons because of it. I ignored the obvious foolishness of his thinking that there was a singular accent in any nation, let alone one so vast and diverse. Anyhow, I'd been running an online ad for a few weeks and had no shortage of people willing to pay cash for English lessons. Then again, they were all men and I was too naive at that point to realize what was wanted of me. It was no different from when I've lived alone elsewhere in the world, but for some reason my guard was down in Korea.

The adoptees and I were at another barbecue place. It was a large group and most of us lived at the guesthouse together. I'd joined in because I didn't want to be alone at night, even though, as a vegetarian, I was outside their dining community. That American boasted about his Korean brother, the one he had just met a few days earlier, not noticing the tense smiles around the table as those who hadn't made connections, who felt hopeless about ever finding anyone in Korea who knew them or remembered them, patiently listened to his good fortune. I'd seen this dynamic play out many times. We fell into two camps: the reunited and the still-searching. Of course, there were people who said they didn't care, that they were not looking. Maybe they weren't. So I suppose there were three groups. But this division was one of the things that made the guesthouse such a broken place. When we were around other adoptees, how could we express our joy and fear and anger at our Korean families when there were others without? That American adoptee failed to notice, or acknowledge, or care about the sorrow of his fellow diners. With his mouth full of bulgogi, he told me to move my separately ordered dish to the centre of the table so everyone could have some, dipping his spoon into my bowl of vegetables, tofu, and rice. For reasons I still can't comprehend today, I complied.

The mosquitoes in Korea were different, smaller and darker and louder. Their bites burned and swelled hard pebbles under my skin. I still have scars on my arms and legs from that first trip, when my blood was as novel to them as their viciousness was to me. Every room of the guesthouse, especially where people slept, had plug-in repellents wafting chemical steam into the air. But they didn't work, so each night the lights would be abruptly flashed on whenever the humming grew unbearable and adoptees from around the world, assigned bunk beds with strangers, would stomp around the room, swearing in French and German and English and Norwegian, swinging electric bug zappers like tennis rackets.

In late September, Ummah took me and Bora by the arm and, for the first and only time, went home for the holidays with her two daughters. We visited the school where she'd been a student as a young girl. We inspected the well that provided water to the entire family. My grandfather showed off the small plot of grapevines that was their livelihood. Still wearing his indoor slippers, he offered to take me on a tour of the town on the back of his moped, handing me the construction worker's hat he used in lieu of a proper helmet, but Ummah said *absolutely not*.

We slept together on the floor of my grandparents' one-room house in Gimcheon. Halabuji's television droned throughout the night. They must have worked quietly, Ummah and Halmoni, to make a Chuseok breakfast over electric hot plates and open fire, waking at four or five in the morning, because everything was laid out at sunrise. I'd learn later that it was tradition to celebrate annual harvest time like this, not just in my family but in many other Korean families too. I learned that Chuseok was a holiday that was spent with family. That more Koreans travelled home for Chuseok than for Christmas and New Year celebrations combined.

They'd made songpyeon, sweet rice cake dumplings steamed on pine needles. They'd made many of them. But I was not yet accustomed to the sweetness, to the texture of that food, and so I tried only a little. Halmoni sat in one corner of the house eating a hard persimmon. Ummah didn't insist when I refused dish after dish. My grandfather ate nothing and said nothing, but sipped soju by himself. Every now and then I'd catch him staring at me, and he wouldn't look away but would gaze directly into my eyes. His thick eyebrows made him look stern. Without words, that's all there was.

I'd see my grandparents once more that autumn. The next time I visited Korea, I stood in front of Halabuji's grave, unsure of what to do. Still with nothing to say. Still sitting with his silence.

Before she lived in northern India for however many months, and before she toured the rest of the country with her boyfriend on their holiday from the perfume farms in Australia, Bora sat next to me in a near-empty theatre in Seoul and watched a heartbreaking Sanjay Leela Bhansali film captioned in Korean. She wondered why I didn't cry at the right times, and we laughed when she realized that I understood neither the Korean subtitles nor the Hindi language spoken by the actors. I promised her I didn't mind. I didn't tell her, but I'd been watching her the entire time anyway.

In the letter she'd sent before I came to Korea, Bora listed the things she wanted to do together once I arrived. *Tell secrets. Watch a film.* She described how jealous she'd been of friends who had older sisters. We saw each other every few weeks, meeting to eat ice cream or drink coffee, even though she was busy with her many jobs and her studies. She had also started English language classes, but back then she didn't want anyone to know. Bora always chose restaurants she thought I'd like: Mexican, Italian, Indian, American. One night, after she ate too much dairy, she was sick in the public restroom of a state-of-the-art shopping mall. She let me rub her back. Hold her hair. I bought her ginger candy and brought her water.

We met often and spent time, without talking, discovering each other through the slightest expressions.

44

We developed an intimacy without the burden of words. Bora always insisted on paying and I later discovered that Ummah gave her money so that her two daughters could build a connection. So we could learn to be sisters.

My mother asked me often if I'd like to go to the public baths with her. I'd read about Korean spas in a tour book. I knew that I was expected to be naked because the saunas she proposed were not coed. That I should wash my mother, scrub her skin, her hair. That I should let her do the same to me. I hope someone told her that Westerners can be more private about their bodies. I hope she didn't think it was because of her that I felt distant. But maybe it was. I'm still afraid to see her unclothed body. The soft skin of her midsection. Gentle rolls of fat. The breasts of a woman who nursed two of her three children. That body has become foreign to me and I'm scared to see it. If she hadn't noticed the vast cultural space between us up to that point, my refusal to ever accept her invitation to the baths must have confirmed it. She eventually registered that I could never be the kind of Korean daughter she'd fully be able to recognize.

Ummah bought me a cellphone and a metrocard that she refilled without my knowledge. But I was afraid to take the subway at night because the routes were too complicated and, especially when I was tired, the recorded Korean audio announcing the stations was indecipherable. To get to the guesthouse I had to make a connection and ride a public bus for a short while. When Ummah learned that I often took taxis after dark, the way I would anywhere else in the world, she asked the agency worker, she asked Bora, and she asked someone at the guesthouse to insist that I not. They told me it wasn't safe. Not for someone who doesn't speak Korean. Not for a woman travelling alone. Those small acts of care. Although Ummah wasn't physically next to me, even though she couldn't be there to watch over me, I felt her protecting me in the ways she could.

One night it was far too late to take the metro back from the bar in Hongdae. The other adoptees were drunk. I'd been drinking too. Earlier that night, a white man ran up to me while we were all seated together. He was completely naked. We ignored him because it didn't seem unusual. By then I'd grown accustomed to how foreigners behave in those spaces. I'd learned to avoid white men in military fatigues. I never went to Itaewon alone. I was tired. Remembering Ummah's fear that a taxi driver would harm me if I rode alone, I asked another adoptee if he'd accompany me back to the guesthouse. We spoke French because he'd been raised in a small town outside Paris. We'd not known each other long, but he seemed sober enough, and the fact that I could speak to him in his first language offered what I thought was an instant connection. I was relieved when he agreed. I said it was because I was afraid to try to find my way home by myself. But inside the taxi, he started to touch me and I grew sad that there is never a place or a person with whom to feel safe.

I spoke to my Canadian parents on videophone while I was in Seoul. The Internet connection wasn't great and there wasn't any privacy at the guesthouse, so our conversations were always short. The time difference didn't help. They were worried about me being alone in Korea. They were worried about themselves too, I'm sure. When I told them how good it felt to be in a land of people who looked like me, how my heart was beating differently now, my mother left the room because she was upset. I understood that she was afraid I'd want to stay. In truth, part of me wanted to. And they couldn't see themselves ever travelling to that place. I pondered how curious it is that Korea is imagined as so close when we're being taken away, infants alone on airplanes, but so far when we want to return.

The other adoptees felt like celebrating even when there was nothing to celebrate. Late into the night, nearly every night, they offered toasts, crashing together beer glasses and soju bottles bought for one U.S. dollar at the convenience store. The guesthouse became an alternate universe where the pressures of holding everything in, caretaking everyone else's emotions, faded away. So maybe that's what they were celebrating: the freedom to live alongside so many others who could relate to them in that one meaningful way. It was a place where their needs, our needs, were central.

I moved from upstairs into the basement because I needed to work. I was finishing a thesis about adoption from Asia, but my research was stalled. Concentration left me and I wrongly believed solitude was the answer. The single-occupancy apartment downstairs had a twin bed with a bare mattress, a reading light clipped to the headboard, and a desk. Maybe there was also a dresser, but I can't remember. I tucked two fitted sheets onto the bed because there were tiny bugs crawling in the seams of the mattress. Of course, living down there meant I separated myself from the other people at the guesthouse. And sometimes I'd be jealous of their connections with one another. But the quiet appealed to me. It cost me a lot, though, that silence.

I met Ummah at a restaurant in a neighbourhood I no longer recall. It was dark when I arrived and she was with another woman. Around her age. When I joined them, Ummah took my hand in hers the way she sometimes did and the other woman began to cry. That woman touched me, my face, my hair, and I let her. Her hands were small birds fluttering, fast wings, sweeping a hair here, feathering a cheekbone there. Somehow I knew, without being told, she needed proof of me, and her fingertips offered that. I was bewildered by how quickly they, she and Ummah, spoke. How they laughed. That my mother was drinking beer, something I'd never witnessed her doing. She seemed lighter, which was also something I'd never before seen.

The ajumma spoke some English to me. She complimented me as pretty and youthful, and Ummah, forgoing social custom, agreed by her silence. By her refusal to refuse. Then the woman I'd just met handed me an envelope with hundreds of thousands of won, and a box with a designer scarf inside. *Mommy's daughter comes home*, she pronounced carefully in English. A few days later I found out she was my mother's childhood friend. She was the only other person who'd known my mother was pregnant. Who knew I'd gone away.

The window of the fifth-floor hotel room we'd rented for the weekend bowed towards the ocean, overlooking Haeundae Beach. It was mid-October and there were four of us: the Korean professor who was my connection at the college, one of her students, Ummah, and me. We were in Busan for the annual international film festival. Mats of different colours were folded and piled to one side; later that night, they'd be our beds. The wood floor was already starting to warm and the sea was angry, lunging against and over the straight barriers, surprising drivers as they tried to parallel park. It was two months into my time in Korea, and dusk, so the ashes of a hundred fireplaces swarmed the air and stuck to people's hair like flakes of dead skin. Without daylight savings, autumn in Korea meant extraordinary darkness.

At the time, I didn't really consider the risk my mother took in coming on that weekend trip, but it must have been high. It was the second occasion we would sleep together the way mothers and daughters in Korea do. It had seemed like a good idea when, back in Seoul a few weeks earlier, the professor proposed the small vacation. When it was happening, though, I was bored by Korean conversation that kept me apart from the rest of the group. There was a bag of grapes, some cherry tomatoes, a cake, but I stayed to the side of the open room holding a dictionary to my chest and looking out the window.

But then, unprompted, Ummah told the story of my birth. When she started, it was to no one but the unfurnished room. Maybe she was overcome by the need to tell, knowing the professor could hear her, that the student could hear her, and together they could translate her words to me. Maybe it would be her only chance. Our only chance. This is how our kinship has always needed to exist— through third parties. My mother told me about the day I was born, but we needed strangers to bear witness.

I threw away your clothes, she said before anyone was paying much attention. *The clothes I bought before you were born.*

Ummah promised she'd not been ashamed when I was growing inside her. Even though my father was married. Even though he already had one child. A son. Still a baby. He promised we'd be a family instead. Him, Ummah, me. They rented an apartment. I wondered who signed the lease, but I was afraid to interrupt. Now I wish I had. It makes a difference who signed it.

She was in Seoul to work. She was sewing in a factory, as she'd continue to do for decades. As she was doing still when we'd met earlier that year. Her family was in Gimcheon, hours away. Worlds away. She was young. She loved him. He sang to her. His hair was thick with curls. His skin, like hers, was dark and rich. He was taller than most Korean men. He had freckles. He was from the city and she couldn't believe he wanted to love her. And then she didn't believe he ever actually did.

I was afraid to move. I was afraid she'd stop talking. At times I looked out the window, but it was pitch-black and I saw only our reflections mirrored back. I was holding my breath. She was holding my hand.

Another baby came. My sister. Unni. Also with his wife. She must look like her mother, because she doesn't look like our father, she doesn't look like me. He lived between homes, sometimes with his already-born children, sometimes with my mother. And then, only a few months later, I arrived.

It was early morning. She remembered that. Her parents were there. I was quiet. She'd been dreaming of persimmon and rock fruit during her pregnancy, so she knew I'd be a girl. She swore the room filled with the smell of iron and cinnamon when I emerged. My father was there. His parents were there. None of them looked at her. None of them looked at me. Panicked because she remembered the stress of her pregnancy, my mother scanned me, counting every finger, every toe, rolling each one between her index finger and thumb.

Then, in the hallway, my grandfather was talking to someone Ummah didn't know. Then he was talking to his son, my father. Then he slapped his son, my father, across the face and walked away. Then my father walked away too.

I couldn't breathe. The professor was crying as she translated Ummah's words. The student was also crying.

The stranger came into the birthing room. She had papers in her hand. Someone lifted me from Ummah's arms. The stranger said something about a God Ummah wouldn't know until decades later. Something about doing the right thing. Something about the future.

The story slowed to a stop around there. The waves of tension and pain broke. There was nothing else to say. Exhaustion rushed in. But when it was done, Ummah held on to me, awkward because we were two grown women seated on the floor, so our legs got in the way. She held my hand still. She offered me her breast, something she'd not thought of or hadn't the time for when first she bore me into the world. I declined, saddened. Most of what'd been told didn't register in the moment. It would come back to me in memory later. Because early on, something my mother said triggered three words that repeated blood-pulse and thunder in my head. Louder than my history and my mother's life secrets unfurling, spread out immodestly in front of strangers. Louder than the still-raging ocean. Water breaking hard. Then pressure. Then pain that could split a woman in two. Then quiet awe at what had just happened. That night, I cried in front of my mother at last. When she stopped speaking and the room vibrated, those three words fell from my mouth, over and over. The only thing I'd say in response to her telling. *You wanted me.*

Unni . . . I have to whisper this because if I say it aloud everything is going to fall down onto me and I'll be buried so deep no one will ever find me. There have been so many men who have taken a part of me, taken it away without permission, that I can't even count. You went to college too? Did you live in a dorm with floormates who checked the doors as they walked down the hall and, finding one unlocked, thought they could enter that space and any person living there without asking? And have you ever woken up with someone on top of you, inside you, but you were unable to open your eyes or move your arms or legs? Unable to move your mouth, so your silence became your surrender? I hope not. But the worst happened not long before you and I first met, unni. One night, at the adoptee guesthouse in Seoul, about a month after I'd moved from upstairs and into that basement apartment, I was held down by another broken person who tried to put himself together by pulling me apart. He tore through me, hardened by my black eyes looking out the window, wet and away from his face. In me he hated and loved the Korean mother who, when he was three, didn't even bother to pin his name and birthdate to his shirt when she told him she would be right back. When she disappeared into the crowd, determined, dreaming his future as well as her own.

He came away from me with the salt of my blood on the tip of his tongue. A handful of hair accidentally snapped off because who would have thought I'd be so breakable. So poorly made. He came away with immediate softness maybe contracted from my own body that went limp under his hands. Rabbit pelt slung over one arm.

I wanted to leave. The guesthouse. Korea. My body. Everything. I wanted to run away, but I had nothing and no one to run towards. I'd paid for my housing at the beginning of my stay, in cash, so I had no extra funds. I knew how to make quick money back home, but I was afraid in Korea, where I didn't have a sure footing and where I'd already been vanished once before. I hesitated too long and then it started to feel foolish to not just carry on the way I'd always done. There was nothing exceptional about that time in the guesthouse basement, besides the fact that I was shocked when it happened. I thought I was harder than that. More seeing, at least.

Today, still, that night comes back to me.

The moon glowed enough light through the glass exterior doors of the basement walk-out that I could see the vague outline of the table in the centre of the room, the out-of-tune piano off to one side. I was wearing a blue pullover—one of two I bought in a metro station because I'd not been prepared for the dampness of Korean fall. It was around four in the morning and I left my basement apartment. I felt my way across the large meeting space towards the toilet. I could see his silhouette stumbling down the pathway to the basement instead of in the direction of the main house. I stopped. He had a key. I held my breath. He was given privileges to use that space too, or had them before I started living down there. No one thought to ask for the key back. He saw me even though it was dark and I stood frozen like a rabbit, unblinking. I'd noticed him watching me at our shared meals. He was too attentive. In hindsight, I knew him. I knew what he was going to do.

He bit my mouth. I didn't make a sound. The moonlight dipped into the acne scars on his cheeks. Strings of saliva sailed down from his lips onto my neck. My face. I looked through the glass pane of the exterior door.

The next day, I was moved into the main quarters to a shared room with an adoptee from Denmark. We were friends and I told her. Still today, she remembers his name, but I ask her not to say it aloud. I didn't have the words to tell many others. His actions were rationalized by the few people to whom I confessed. He was drunk. It's hard for adoptees to return to Korea. His girlfriend had left him. It wasn't the first time I was encouraged to keep quiet because my words would damage an already traumatized community. People asked me, *what do you imagine Koreans will think of returning adoptees if you tell anyone about this? Who will help us if this comes out?*

Anyway, I had no one to translate for me. I know it could have been much worse. So when I saw him the next week and he insisted we talk privately about what had happened, I told him it was fine, that I understood why I needed to forget it. I know part of me pushed it aside because it is always humiliating, sitting through those conversations after the fact. I'm ashamed, of course. And a coward. But I didn't have it in me at the time to do anything more than collect myself back together again. Now, years later, when insomnia is particularly bad, I can still remember the stitched design on the pockets of his jeans as he walked away from me and that thing he did.

In that adoptee guesthouse we were supposed to come together as imagined family and pray. But if I am like your sister and you are like my brother, then why were you using my body, my dignity, to express your anger over the country and culture that cut us both loose decades ago? Why did my body have to be the place where you dug for comfort? What did you find inside me, where I live? Peace? Relief? The frozen, dead centre of a mother who, rumour has it, left you at a train station when you were three? The hollow bones of a magpie stripped of its black and blue feathers, crushed to powder under the weight of it all?

Three months or so after I first arrived in Seoul, my Korean father introduced himself to me in a text message. By then I had been waiting for him to impose himself one way or another. The agency gave him my phone number. They'd told him I was in Seoul, a worker admitted by email. I don't remember exactly how it went, but they warned me that he knew. I figured he would call me in the middle of the night or maybe show up at the doorstep of the guesthouse with a sheet cake and flower arrangement. Eventually he did those things, as if we were in some awkward courtship and he was wooing me with generic grocery store gifts. But first there was the text message.

It didn't come as much of a surprise because, from the stories I had heard about him from Ummah, from my imo, and a little bit from Halmoni, this was the way he operated. He launched himself into people's lives when their guard was down and messed things up, and then sulked if anyone had the courage to look him in the eye and tell him he wasn't as great as he thought he was.

The actual words of the text message I don't remember. I asked a volunteer at the guesthouse to explain them to me, even though by then I had a pretty good idea of what was being said. I needed a witness, not a translator, which is why I showed that person. It said something to the effect of: *Hello, Heijun. I am your father.* He said he missed me and wanted to meet me. I think I agreed because I was worried that the high of my homecoming was starting to wear off. And then I'd only have the lows of my return to sit with. I'd been climbing and climbing, and I was afraid of things levelling once the thrill of reunion ended. Worse yet, I was afraid of the necessary fall.

We met, Ummah and I, at the guesthouse and then took the metro in silence until we reached Yeoksam station. She held my hand when we entered the adoption agency, this time together. My father was already in the room. Maybe it was the room I'd been in before. I don't know. They all look the same. He was wearing a suit and, as Ummah'd done in August, he ran to me and held on tight. Folded himself around me. Again, my body turned hard and my eyes searched the room while he cried into my hair. He didn't acknowledge my mother, who was now seated on one of the couches, maybe watching, maybe looking away.

He did most of the talking. The translator recounted the many times over the years that he'd visited the agency trying to get access to me. To find out my name and where I lived. How they'd turned him away again and again. How he'd been promised I'd been raised in Korea, so he hired a private detective who searched all over the country. At some point in his telling he noticed that Ummah held my hand and seemed to register where my heart was. His eyes narrowed even though he smiled with all his teeth and laughed his lion's laugh.

He stopped when I started to cry. For all those months in Korea, besides that one night in Busan, I'd walled my sadness and anger into my body, so my organs were full and my skin hurt from the tension. But there, at the agency where it'd all started, a small crack appeared and everything came rushing out. My father flinched when I pointed a finger in his face. He got up to leave when I said that at last I'd met my mother but because of his actions years ago I couldn't even talk to her. *Because of you*, I said, *we cannot speak. We have nothing.* The social worker refused to translate. I was spoiling another reunion, though differently this time. It didn't matter. She didn't need to tell him the meaning behind my anger. It was the first of many times my father and I would communicate through emotion, through pain, not words.

Ummah held me and I think she knew where my grief was coming from. Maybe she understood that I was trying to say what she could not. Soon I'd leave Korea, and I had nothing to lose. That time, he stayed and took it. That time, he forgave me for blaming him. Not that I asked for his forgiveness.

What I didn't know back then was that Ummah and my father had spoken on the phone once, before the reunion at the agency. She'd contacted him when she learned of his text message. How does one speak to a former lover, twenty-seven years after everything has fallen away? The man who walked out without looking back?

We left the agency in mid-afternoon and my father drove us first to a noraebang, where I watched my parents sing together, where my father bought a tray of overpriced cold cuts that went untouched because I didn't eat meat and Ummah didn't like to either. Like other older men I'd known, he postured wealth and power in ways that drew me in. After the noraebang, we visited one of the shops he owned and he dressed me like a doll in polyester clothes that were sizes too big. He showed me off to his sister, my gomo, to a man who may have been my uncle. We ate Korean food for dinner, and he stirred my bibimbap and held the spoon to my mouth, feeding me all night. Encouraged more and more as our time together went on, he sang songs, lifted me into the air, and tried to kiss me on the mouth. Ummah laughed. I wondered if she recognized those moves from when he courted her decades earlier. At some point, my mother stopped holding my hand and took my father's arm instead. They started to act as though I was the child they'd lost long ago. They sang, *oo-ri ddal, our daughter,* while pinching me all over. It was exciting and horrifying at once.

I thought, if Ummah can forgive him, maybe I should too. And I thought, since he already knows about me, and since—unlike her current boyfriend—he wants me, he is the man who will allow me to have an open relationship with my mother. He will make me legitimate in this place. And I thought, maybe we can make-believe we're a regular family at least for a little while. A family with a baby trapped in the body of a nearly thirty-year-old woman. I thought, what further harm could we inflict on each other? Sometimes I thought, what can I get out of this man? What does he owe us, Ummah and me? But that was just me trying to convince myself I knew what I was doing.

Predictably, it turned out that he was always the one asking for things. Even when he was giving me things —clothes and cookies and little-girl tea sets bought on the side of the road that I would eventually display next to one of my Canadian grandmothers' bone china cup-and-saucers—he was also asking for something. He wanted respect. He wanted adoration. He wanted a daughter who would worship him, because he'd messed things up with my older sister, who, I later learned, was barely speaking to him then. He wanted absolution. Forgiveness. But I was never the person to give it. Even if I was, I thought, it was going to cost him more than he could afford.

In the meantime, I let him slip me years' worth of envelopes stuffed with won that I on purpose wasted on makeup. I let him feed me with his hands, write my name in the sand at the beach, carry me like a baby on his back or like a new bride in his arms. I saw ours in the same way I did other relationships with older men whom I knew wanted something from me. I took what I could and rationalized with myself that I was in charge. He offered me a car. A house. A kitten. He spoiled me, and eventually I started to forget myself. I started to soften. Later, when I returned home to Canada, he would call every morning, the Internet phone he'd couriered to our Montreal apartment playing a childish melody, letting me know it was time for me to transform back into a giggling daddy's girl, cinnamon and sugar. I regressed to the baby I had been when his own selfishness prompted his family to sign the papers that would throw me across the ocean with a safety belt carving a line in my skin, my body erupting in what a doctor described as the worst case of diaper rash he'd ever seen, because no one checked on me during the trans-Pacific flight. With each phone call the memory of that deep scar started to let up, things began to feel real, and I'll admit I lost control of myself. I lost my anger for a moment. When he asked, *do you love me?* I promised I did. When he asked me to count to ten in Korean, I obeyed. When he asked, *what noise does a puppy make?* I barked on command. I started to call him Appah—Father—and to think of him that way too.

Unni . . . How did he, our father, tell you about me? You probably thought I was much younger, a result of the affair that led him to abandon you and your mother when you were a teenager. Did he tell you about the first few months of your life, when he went between your family's apartment and my mother's bed? That those same hands that gently turned your head so it could be shaved not long after the seaweed soup and rice cakes were eaten, the next day caressed the swollen belly of a woman who knew another daughter would soon arrive because she nightly dreamed persimmons? Did they tell you together, your mother and our father, reuniting after all those years to confess my name and what they let happen to me? I know, when you found out, you insisted we should have been raised together, one girl only slightly smaller but notably darker and skinnier than her sister. But did you wonder why I had to be tossed away, first to an orphanage and then to a land so far from anyone's imagination? Did you ask who agreed to my mother's punishment for our father's infidelity? Unni, did they tell you that blocks away from your own nursery was another, made ready for a sister who never arrived? Whom they said had died? That my mother threw away the clothes I would never wear?

My father was proud of his dated sedan because it was a Ford. The stereo was old, without even a CD option, but it didn't matter because he only listened to sports broadcasts in the car. My mother also was proud, sitting in the front seat as if she was used to being in a car, let alone a foreign one. Bora was to my right in the back seat. She slept for most of the drive, her head bent at a frightening angle. Broken-necked bird.

No one bothered to tell me the name of the village. The exterior of the cabin looked small, but it was large enough indoors. There were trees all around that were already bare. It was late November. The leaves were slippery on the ground, fish scales of every colour, glossed with their own decay. The sweetness of forest decomposition was thick. It was night by the time we arrived. We had no luggage, only food we'd bought along the way. Kimbap, wrapped tight in plastic that was peeled back like the skin of a banana. Individually packaged cakes that looked and tasted like the ones I used to share with my Canadian sister growing up, one girl dividing, the other choosing first. Bora fitted one cake with a candle and everyone sang together, unconcerned that actually it was no one's birthday at all.

At night we slept on the floor like a family. Under one blanket. On top of one mat. I woke up panicked, gasping, because of something I didn't have the words to explain, and even if I'd had, no one would have understood me.

That night, Ummah clasped my father's hand and shook it in the air as though they'd won a race. They repeated, *ga-jok, family*, like it was a victory chant. Bora bit her lip and looked out the window at the naked tree branches.

It must have happened that Ummah left her boyfriend and my father left his girlfriend—or wife, I was never clear—because all of a sudden they were always together. Ummah was free to see me whenever she wanted. They expected me every day. As December came around, they became a regular presence at the guesthouse, always appearing unannounced. I asked them not to come. I saw the faces of those adoptees who were still searching.

I wondered if my mother had to convince herself that she was making the right decision, as sometimes I did in my twenties when a particular lover was almost, but not quite, good enough. Also, I wondered if they fell again into the pattern of a relationship put on hold for three decades. Or if it was brand new. And they told themselves that theirs was the kind of remarkable love that is true and deep and lasting. When I told people back in Canada that my Korean parents had re-found each other, they marvelled at the novelty. Friends who had no way of knowing how unsteady it all felt imagined me celebrating life righting itself. But I always knew the risk, the danger, of what was unfolding. I felt the pressure rising with each day. I couldn't stop it. I just looked on, the tension vibrating across my skin, and waited for the blow that would break us apart again.

Unni . . . Do you remember when our father introduced us at that amusement park, bringing us together to do little-girl things even though we were nearly thirty at the time? He broke off pieces of pancake and, with his fingers, put them directly into our mouths. We dressed up in hanboks and awkwardly held on to each other with hands placed stiffly on silk-covered waists. We rode the children's train while our father ran after us taking photos. I didn't know that you'd been estranged from him for years before that day. Did he use me to lure you back into his life in the same way he promised you to me?

Unni, we have the same hands. Everyone back home noticed when I showed them photographs of us together. That day at the park, you bought me cookies and ice cream and cake and spaghetti. You gave me trinkets I still keep safe. I guess you were trying to make up for decades of missed birthdays and New Years, not that anyone blames you. You grew up as the youngest in your family. You'd never had a sister. You asked if I liked your blouse, if you should grow out your bangs, fussing your collar with your eyebrows raised and an inquisitive nod. Miming scissors with your fingers because we shared no common language. Later, when it was time for me to go back to Canada, you took advantage of your job at Incheon International and waited with me at the gate after buying me Chanel makeup at duty-free. You stuffed a loaf of bread into my carry-on luggage for no reason other than to feed me on that long journey. When it arrived with me in Montreal, we were both flattened. I ate it anyway.

I left behind a box of grape juice in the common area of the guesthouse. Inside were fifty individual sacs, swollen like eggs, with grainy red-black liquid. Holding them was holding my blood. Our blood. It amazed me.

I left it behind after I'd been hiding it all those months I lived in the adoptee guesthouse. I left it because my suitcase was filled with cheap acrylic sweaters and ornamentalism and nail polish. Maybe part of me left it because it didn't belong back in Canada. We don't have grapes like that.

I had been storing it under a pile of blankets I'd bought from vendors in the metro station. My parents too bought me new bedding one afternoon after they came and cleaned the guesthouse. *It's normal*, Bora explained, *for parents to clean their children's rooms.*

The grape juice had been a gift from my grandparents. Bagged juice from their small farm. I could taste in it something rich. But it tasted too much, it was too intense. So I stopped.

I only drank it that one time. It stained my lips. I only needed to drink it once, because I'll never forget how it tastes.

My mother waited in the car while Appah helped me choose flowers for the guesthouse owners. And then, with my luggage in the trunk, we left for the airport together. It was mid-December and there was some snow. Bora was working, so it was just the three of us riding in silence.

The airport appeared too quickly, and too quickly I was checked in. Unni met us there, scheduling her lunch break for when we arrived. She had clearance to come with me right onto the airplane, which she did, covering me with a blanket before touching the side of my face with her fingers. But even before that, Ummah cried and Appah did too when we had to separate. I cried because even though I was eager to return to Canada, I felt the weight of that decision. I said something as we parted about the time I'd left Korea as a baby. How it hadn't been my choice. How my heart was breaking leaving now because this time it was. More empty sounds without meaning. That day, though, unlike the first time I left, my parents kissed me goodbye.

After four months in Korea, I returned to Canada, and the Internet phone would ring every morning around eight o'clock. It was the end of the workday in Korea and I could hear the exhaustion in my parents' voices. Ummah would tell me she was making my father the same Korean soup I had eaten nearly every day in Seoul. They lived together by then. She'd laugh, almost apologetically, confessing that it would be the same meal as the previous night and the night before. I sometimes wondered if she was actually cooking different things but knew I only recognized the names of a few dishes.

She'd ask me if I'd eaten, and each time I'd say, *I don't want to eat. I want to stay thin.* I said it to tease her because I knew she worried, but actually it was more than all that. For years I'd struggled with food disorders, loving the way I could interlace my fingers between my ribs when I wrapped my arms around myself. Loving the feeling of control that came with it. Sometimes I slept with my forearms hooked neatly in the arches of hip bones that stuck out just a little bit too much. Ummah begged me to eat something and I always promised I would, but I didn't. Hunger made me feel connected to my body and in control of what was happening around me. Back in Canada, I was floating up again, bit by bit. I noticed that no matter where I was in the world, I was always missing somewhere else. I felt unsettled. Hunger held me together.

The phone would be passed to my father. He wanted me to see myself as his daughter, to name myself after him. To announce myself Shim Heijun, so I jokingly proclaimed myself Kim, after my mother's family. He always asked me if I knew who he was. He wanted absolution and he acted as though, if I repeated his name day after day, it would make it so. He called me *ddal*, daughter, with its aggressive consonant beginning and almost swallowed conclusion. Sometimes he asked me to sing nursery rhymes line by line, following his lead. When I finished, he'd sing a cheer.

Appah was the first person to call me aloud by my Korean name as if I had no other. Everyone else followed: Ummah. Unni. He'd opened the door for them. Felt entitled to erase, without hesitation, my other name and, with it, my other identity. At the time, I liked the novelty of it. Later I saw it as his refusal to admit that I had been raised in Canada. His refusal to accept blame. Or to see who I had become.

Today, when I call her, Ummah always gasps before she says my name, as though she's surprised that I've contacted her. Then she laughs. The people closest to me, even in Canada, call me by my Korean name.

Early in 2010, I met a Québécois man who'd also been adopted from Korea. We were both registered in the same Korean language class at a community centre near Atwater station. He'd not made contact with family but was hopeful and had been back to Korea many times. He was a wanderer. I saw in him the many broken people I'd lived with at the guesthouse, but he was the first adoptee raised in Canada with whom I'd share meaningful conversation. I may have been his first, too.

I can say, because it is fact, that he and I were the worst students in the class. Not only that, but technically we were the only Koreans there too, clumsily sounding out an alphabet so foreign and definitely not inherited. Seemed everyone else was taking their K-drama obsession to the next level, or cramming before a year-long teaching gig in Busan, or trying to find a girlfriend in time for the Fantasia film fest. Madame Kwon zeroed in on us, wanting us to succeed. We confused her when we didn't. Upset her belief that the Korean spirit is so powerful that it can overcome anything. I mean, were we so different from all those Koreans who'd burst out of Japanese colonialism, tongues naturally ready for pepper paste *and* their beloved, outlawed language?

We responded to our shortcomings differently. I studied harder, fell back into the Protestant ethic I'd been raised on, filling exercise books with rows and rows of dictation. My friend, he slacked off. Drifted through the two-hour classes obviously drunk. Didn't show up the week we were supposed to give ten-minute oral presentations. I get it, though. It felt bad to see our language blossom so effortlessly in the mouths of non-Koreans. Hobbyists and Orientalists, while we struggled. It stifled us, our desperation.

For a short while we'd tell each other everything, our lives serialized into ten-minute episodes slotted into class breaks. When I offered stories about my Canadian family and, encouraged by him, my Korean family, he neither hardened nor softened, which is why I always gave him more. He told me things too. How he grew up in a large family, all the children adopted from different countries. It wouldn't be the last time I'd meet someone with a similar childhood. Although he never said so, I know it messed him up. Sometimes he'd arrive uninvited at our apartment with bottles of soju, trying to numb himself with the liquor of our ancestors. Once, I joined him. I remember being so intoxicated that I fell backwards from my chair. My fiancé was so upset that he asked my friend to leave the apartment. But he also was saddened because he saw my friend's grief and didn't know where he'd end up.

Of course, he stopped coming to class after that, the other adoptee. It hurt because I knew it was a place where he was trying, imperfectly, to find something recognizable in himself. But then, because loss was the thread that we'd woven between us, and that pain urged us to hurt ourselves even further, we'd fallen apart. I eventually gave up looking over my shoulder each time the door opened at the back of the classroom; I knew he wouldn't show. There were only three weeks left when Madame Kwon began skipping over his name in roll call. In our final session, weeks after my friend had stopped coming to class, Madame Kwon shook my hand and wished me luck, squinting and smirking. She never understood how a true Korean couldn't learn the language, which made her look for evidence in my face that I wasn't actually who I said I was. That's all I took from that course. That and the fact that she never asked me if I knew what had happened to her other Korean student who'd suddenly vanished.

After I was securely back to my life in Canada, after
everyone here exhaled in relief because I'd returned, Bora
arrived in Montreal, moving into the front bedroom of
our apartment. She'd come to study English, to expand
on the lessons she'd started taking a year earlier after she
learned she had an older sister in Canada. She came to
help me plan my small wedding. She still called me unni
in those days. We cooked together. She wanted to learn
lasagna and hollandaise sauce. Once, we drove to
Ontario and my Canadian family met her and embraced
her without hesitation, but part of me was relieved by the
language barrier there. We had months together before
my Korean parents came for the celebration, and that
time was spent as sisters living together in Montreal. We
walked through the city, holding hands the way we'd
done in Seoul, our roles suddenly reversed as I
protectively watched over her in this foreign place.

It was the first time they'd applied for passports. Their flight arrived so late that, although it was mid-July, their first glimpse of Canada was black sky. Montreal at night is nothing compared with the electricity of Seoul after dark. We'd rented a car knowing they'd never be able to make it by taxi to our apartment in the Village. Bora came with us, her English-Korean dictionary in hand.

When my parents appeared through the doors that block any view of customs and immigration, my mother started her nervous laugh. She ran first to Bora then to me, and then awkwardly half-bowed to, half-hugged my fiancé. My father was pushing a cart piled high with boxes and luggage. He wore a baseball cap and the knock-off athletic wear I'd grow to associate with him, instead of the grey suits he'd worn seven months earlier when we were all getting to know each other in Korea. His warm-up pants were just a little bit too shiny, the material just a little bit too thin. The silkscreened puma was leaping in the wrong direction. He hugged me, shook my fiancé's hand, and instructed us all it was time to go home. Bora spoke quickly with my parents, pausing now and then to translate that I looked skinny, to comment that my hair was still blond. I tried to pick up words where I could, but my family spoke too fast and did not use the formal grammar I'd been studying in Madame

Kwon's class. Even as I gave up trying to understand, I let the sound of the Korean language float around me like a thousand feathers in the wind. And then Montreal suddenly felt like home.

I ran into my bedroom to retrieve a pocket-sized notebook while my mother was washing the vegetables. But really, there were no words to fully describe the way Ummah held a leaf of cabbage in her left hand, bisecting it down its spine mid-air with a cleaver. Ummah was doing it too quickly and she was an impatient teacher. She didn't wait for me before moving on. Lining up the two halves of the cabbage leaf still in the air and back to back with their now-split spines facing up, Ummah swung the knife downward, hacking the leaves into two-inch square patches. I had never seen anything like that. Later, when I tried to teach some people in Winnipeg this inherited recipe and technique, a white woman sliced open her index finger.

The unrefined sea salt felt like wet sand when I reached into the bag, mimicking my mother's actions. We made a layer of leaves in a bowl, pressed down, dusted salt overtop, and repeated at least ten times. In those days I still bit my nails down to the quick, I still tore at my cuticles and peeled the skin off my fingertips. My eyes watered. The salt burned. When the outer leaves were all cut up and sweating in the bowl, Ummah sat on a stool and, giggling, dipped the core of the cabbage into the bag of wet salt and sucked on the tender yellow leaves.

We were making it the easy way. No sugar, no flour. My mother smelled the garlic I'd bought earlier that day and frowned a bit. She said, *jung-guk*, and I admitted it was, in fact, not Korean but Chinese. Still, Ummah minced the garlic with the chives, onions, ginger. We skipped the fish sauce but not the MSG or the chili flakes. We both forwent the plastic gloves that are expressly made for mixing kimchi. By then my hands were numb anyway. My notebook was covered in rusty stains by the time we stuffed the kimchi into a plastic container. When I teach kimchi, when I give over my mother's recipe because it makes me feel more Korean and sometimes the trade-off seems worth it, I use Mason jars instead of actual Korean containers. Non-Koreans find that more charming. More artisanal.

I will make this recipe hundreds of times over the course of my life. And I'll remember always that first time in our Montreal apartment. My mother had promised she would teach me kimchi, and then she did. I remember I carried the cabbage home from the store like a baby in my arms.

He never let her out of his sight. My father didn't interact with us and yet he also never let us be. It didn't register at first, but we were never alone. When Ummah and I would walk at dusk around Parc La Fontaine, he'd join us though he'd rather have been back at the apartment in front of the television, watching sports highlights of teams he didn't know and athletes he'd never heard of. If I asked Ummah to come with me to the pharmacy, he'd invite himself, and they'd speak Korean and I'd end up walking a few paces ahead. When I physically inserted myself between them, linking my arm through Ummah's the way I had in Seoul before Appah was back in the picture, he'd scowl, snort, and mutter something that I didn't understand and that my mother ignored.

When they first arrived in Montreal, my father boasted with money in the ways men like him do. His wallet was always open, he was always putting out his hand to block the rest of us from paying for even the smallest things. But after a few weeks, and once the reality of the exchange rate set in, he had to relent, standing with hands in pockets while another man, his future son-in-law, paid. Worse yet, sometimes I did.

He complained about my night job, angry that I dressed the way I did to work at a nightclub on St-Laurent, coming home after sunrise. It wasn't just the immodest clothes, it was the cash that I carelessly stored in Mason jars, shoeboxes, and jacket pockets around the apartment. Following my wedding, when I begged my mother to leave him, it was those same rolls of bills I pushed into her hands, promising I could take his place. That I could take care of her. She didn't need to rely on him, because she had me.

In the days leading up to my wedding, after they'd been in Montreal a short while, Ummah and Appah offered me a flat brown box the size of a small end table. Inside, the raw silk fabric of the chima was thin gauze, unembellished with embroidery or gold silkscreening. I wondered how they'd guessed at the right size so the skirt hem would just skim the floor in a way that gave the illusion of floating. I wondered also at the choice of colour. I never wore that shade of pink. The jeogori reminded me of the hanbok jacket I'd worn for show-and-tell in elementary school—short, stiff, and with striped sleeves in alternating colours. Laid flat, the jeogori recalled the animal-pelt rugs sold at antique shops across Canada, deflated deer and elk and black bears with their arms spread as though they'd been hurled from the sky and splayed on the ground. Emptied of life. In that moment, I remembered the thrill and terror that filled my chest when, as a girl, I would stroke those pelts like the family dog, feeling under my fingertips the spectre of vertebrae no longer there.

Ummah tied the chima around my sternum, tucking it under my arms and wrapping it around like an apron. Special socks and shoes, not unlike the wooden clogs my Dutch nanny had gifted me when I was young, remained in the box and still have never been worn. My parents expressed no disappointment when I carefully folded the hanbok back into its box and stored it on a shelf in my closet, not once considering it in lieu of the dress I'd already selected for my wedding day. I hope they understood how precious it was, how I wanted to save it for a more important moment.

I wore a different hanbok on my wedding day. A more
modern one. Appah'd given me the money for that dress.
I'd lost weight in the eight months since I'd last had it
fitted in that stall at Dongdaemun marketplace in Seoul.
Ummah tried to tie my modern hanbok tighter, but
apparently an empire waist is not always one-size-fits-all.
There was no jacket to cover my collarbones, and my eyes
were black with anxiety.

The night before, we'd rehearsed. More than the
wedding itself, the stress of those moments was palpable.
I shook with emotion the entire time. It wasn't only the
pressure of marriage, of fashioning new kinship. It was
the meeting of my families, Korean and Canadian and
Québécois, biological and adoptive and future in-laws,
that feathered panic throughout my entire body. For my
fiancé's family, it was the confirmation that he was less
and less one of them, the foreshadowing of the moment
when he'd begin losing his French, when he'd leave
Quebec behind, when he'd choose to raise his own
children as anglophones. His family loves me and I them.
But we know what lies between us. For my two sets of
parents, it was the drawing close of worlds that were
meant never to come together. The performance of
steadiness when all of our greatest fears and insecurities
came face to face. These families met at the rehearsal. I,
with passable French and mediocre Korean, the only
go-between for them all.

My fiancé's parents arrived by car from their home so far east in Quebec that their town smells like the sea. It smells like Korea, but there are no Koreans living there besides the professor and his wife who run the restaurant where they always remember me and remember that I don't speak the language. Each time we visit, she tells me that her daughters live in Montreal, but she doesn't need to—I don't forget either. When we visit Rimouski, strangers stare. When they register my lack of French, realize I don't intend to stay, the relief on their faces is undeniable. My in-laws shook hands with my Canadian parents at the rehearsal. Everyone spoke loudly and nodded at the right times, as if they could understand each other. At the dinner that followed and at the wedding the next day, they were seated at francophone- and anglophone-only tables.

At the rehearsal, I wore the silk dress Ummah'd bought me back in Seoul, in Insadong on our second day together. She didn't mention it, but she must have noticed. The minister drew me away, and in those few quick moments my Canadian parents approached Ummah and Appah. My Korean parents brought gifts. I missed the exchange. Soon after, I saw Ummah bowing, Appah repeating gratitude through that grin he'd make when he spoke to white people in fractured English. An expression that made me burn with shame, not because of him but because of the people who enjoyed his bowing so much. No one noticed my horror. Everyone applauded his respectful manners. His sing-songed *Thank yous*.

At our wedding, my Korean family and Canadian family stood next to one another, not speaking, but together. We were all together. I told myself I was happy. But I was sick all night. *It means good luck*, people promised in their many languages, when the clouds gathered the day of the wedding. When the rain fell.

The day after my wedding, Bora came to me with something our mother had told her. *Your father won't leave her alone,* she whispered. *He never lets her have any privacy.* I discovered that, back home, he kept her from going to church. He woke her in the middle of the night accusing her, if she'd turned on her side, of dreaming of another man. The Montreal apartment closed in around us as Bora and I begged Ummah to leave my father. To choose us instead of him. My anger and fear and sadness reminded Bora of what she'd witnessed between our mother and her own father. Sometimes she'd let slip pieces of a fractured childhood. But mostly she tried to keep it hidden.

Of her own father, who had also treated our mother horribly, Bora once admitted, *I prayed to Buddha and the Christian God and everyone else. I prayed he would die.* The day after my wedding, the same thought crossed my mind about my own father.

Did he tell you about that night in Montreal, unni? Did he tell you how everything came crashing down and what we'd suspected to be true was, even as we'd hoped it wouldn't be? That there was no putting us back together after all? Did Appah tell you how the apartment walls shook when he yelled at me? How they shook some more when I yelled back? How he was both frightening and not because the undershirt he wore exposed just how big and how old he was at the same time?

The way he treated my mother . . . did he do the same to yours? Bora told me he was jealous. I saw it with my own eyes at the reception when he scowled at Ummah, blaming her each time a man acknowledged her, complimented her hanbok, congratulated her on her daughter's marriage. He couldn't understand them, so he imagined the worst. Was he jealous of your mother also, unni? The way disloyal people often are? You knew this about him all along, didn't you, unni?

That night in Montreal when the walls shook, I looked him in the face and, with all the rage and sadness of my entire life, once again blamed him for everything. Did you ever show him hate like that? Appah and I, we screamed in different languages. I inferred his accusation that I was a bad Korean daughter. I dug in. I told him I could never be a Korean daughter. Least of all, I would never be his Korean daughter. I told him that it was his fault. I said: Look what I've become.

Do you think he understood what I said? Did he tell you, unni, how I ran out into the night? How my husband and

Bora came too? That we stayed at a friend's house and how, when we returned the next morning, they were gone? Maybe you asked him how they made it to the airport without money, or English, or French. Maybe he complained about the cost of changing their tickets to a much earlier flight. Did he tell you that he left a note that Bora translated aloud? It began, *I'm not a bad man . . .* She never finished reading it because I'd already fallen to the kitchen floor. All around me was the blond hair I tore out in fistfuls. From far away, I heard myself screaming in a voice I didn't know: *They've left me again.*

They call people like me, people like us, damaged. *You're broken*, they say, and they shake their heads, sadly, watching us waste our lives trying to find our Korean parents, brothers, sisters, anyone. They witness us handing over our DNA to private companies that boast vast databases and so offer a slim possibility of making connections between biological kin. They see us become wanderers in our birth country, sailing from guesthouse to guesthouse, bleeding a trail of money and self-esteem from one corner of the country to another. They write books about how we storm adoption agencies and grab at files that are neither our own nor in a language we can read. They laugh at how we fall down drunk and convince ourselves that sleeping with others who are there for the same reason is part of our therapy. They purse their lips and roll their eyes when we let Korean men fuck us even though we can't pronounce their names and know we'll never see them again. *Daddy issues*, they smirk.

2.

가지다. Gah-jee-dah.

To have. To take.

<   <   <

All I ever wanted was everything. And for a moment I had it. They'd come back into my life one by one, trying to mortar between cracks with the same hopeful logic that tells us that bones grow stronger at the site of a fracture. But then they disappeared all at once. I was stunned by how sudden it all was.

A bruise settled over my entire body. Swollen blood trauma, trapped by skin, feathering out for everyone to see. Eventually, it faded. But the memory of that time will always be there. Internal bleeding.

I didn't think twice about going to Ontario after my Korean parents left. The day after they left. My new husband, Bora, and I drove ten hours to the place where I grew up and which was the only place I could be in that moment. But even that wasn't where I needed to be. There's nowhere for me to be. That became clearer than it had ever been.

We didn't talk about what had happened, but my Canadian family drew us in and claimed Bora as their third girl. She didn't understand their words, thankfully. Because that's not what she needed then and, I know from my own mistakes, it's not what she's ever needed. I also knew as it was happening that, by letting them in even a little, I was creating the possibility for my family in Ontario to openly express their animosity for my Korean parents, which looked like protectiveness but was really an outlet for their own fears. I know this because I've seen it happen over and over with other people. I'm ashamed to admit I've also bought into that alibi myself.

But when my Korean parents left, I didn't know what else to do. So that's where we went. I never believed in honeymoons anyway.

While we waited for the pumpkin to roast in the oven, Bora and I sat side by side on the grey living room couch. Eventually we ran out of things to say. I was annoyed to find myself filling the quiet by tittering away about nothing the way my mother always felt the need to do. The conversation lapsed and we turned our attentions to the dogs sitting on our respective laps.

She sometimes ran away, you know. Bora made a confession. *When I was growing up, I remember she would leave us for days at a time. She'd fight with my father and she'd leave. I'm not sure where she went. But in a few days she'd come back. It was normal. It happens in a lot of people's families.*

I rolled that idea around in my head while I stroked the dog's ear.

When we returned to Montreal, my arms felt heavy as I stripped my parents' bed. The room smelled stale, like unwashed sheets. I was emotionless when I came across makeshift ashtrays filled with cigarette butts, tucked behind the curtain, a lamp, a pile of books. The water had long ago evaporated, so only yellow-grey residue remained glued to the edges of drinking glasses. I'd asked him not to smoke indoors.

We fell into a rhythm of not mentioning what had happened. But our little home had been broken. My husband whispered explanations to our friends. Warnings that I needed space. As always, he lived around me as I stayed in bed for days. Drank too much. Wrapped my arms around myself and dug into the skin at the back of my neck so deep that there was always dried blood under my fingernails. He came every night with bowls of tea and ointment for my new scratches, wordlessly observing the weight I was losing. Sweeping away piles of used tissues and torn-out hair.

In her own way, Bora stood by me too, saying so much with her eyes and small touches. She'd argued with our mother the night my parents fled Montreal. My sister was crying, but she was angry too. I pieced together some words, whatever I could understand. I think she asked, *why do you always choose men over your children?* Ummah's response something else I could not understand.

When winter came around, I bought a tree and surrounded it with Christmas gifts. With the little money she had, Bora offered me a ring. A candle holder. And a long message, written in English, in a Christmas card: *Sometimes I feel homesick, but I feel better because of you. You make me happy. I wish I could do something for you, but I can do nothing. It makes me sad. I can only study, so I'll study hard and show you my English skills will get better. And don't worry about your Korean parents anymore. Just enjoy your life with me instead. I hope you'll be more happy.*

The card itself was nothing special. The message embossed on the front read: *Across the Miles at Christmas.*

The anniversary of my first arrival in Canada happens in late winter. That date, along with the day I finally returned to Korea, is imprinted in my skin. They hurt. Sometimes, when I was younger, my Canadian parents, probably under the guidance of social workers' advice, would celebrate the anniversary. Sometimes, my Canadian sister would be jealous of the attention. But how can that date be something to memorialize with happiness? I suppose it depends on your perspective: whether it is the anniversary of the time you gained something or the anniversary of the time you lost everything.

For a while, I feared that day as it edged closer each year. Performing happiness and gratitude, and hiding sorrow, also hurts. When January neared its end in 2011, six months after my parents left in the night to go back to Korea, I slowed my breathing on purpose because it was coming faster and faster, my heart was beating louder every day. My husband took me to the outdoor baths that day. In Montreal they're unlike the baths in Korea. But still, he paid a woman who scrubbed my skin until I felt new.

Bora stayed at the apartment and I thought she was studying. But when we arrived home, I saw she'd spent the day preparing a meal of Korean food. She fed me so that I'd not feel loss on that day. And that made me feel new as well.

❧

Sometimes when it was late in Montreal but early in Seoul I'd hear her speaking to our mother on the phone. I never asked my sister what they talked about. From the tone of Bora's voice, everything seemed normal. I couldn't imagine moving on so easily after what happened. But then, my relationship with my Korean family was still so brittle. We didn't have a history of rupture and falling away and then reassembly to assure me that everything would be okay.

At some point, I learned from Bora that our mother and my father had moved to Ummah's hometown of Gimcheon together. That they'd bought a restaurant. I was afraid to ask how my grandparents reacted to his reappearance in Ummah's life, in their lives. Surely they knew it was because I was back in Ummah's life too. That he was there again because of me. My grandfather was dying. My mother likely didn't tell them everything that had happened. How we thought we, Ummah and I, could be closer if she allowed my father back. How, in the end, we were even further apart than before because I was unable to forgive and he was unwilling to change. And because everyone wanted it so much. So when small cracks started to show through, the fragile structure of kinship collapsed all around us.

Appah. Sometimes, when I look in the mirror, I see your face. On my lips. In the shape of my eyes. Down each tangled, curly strand of hair. Across the cheekbones that others covet. In our long jaws. Our arched eyebrows. Our cold, mean stares. The way our lips curl up in the corners. Our smirks. Freckles. Eyelashes. I fucking hate it all.

Bora told me that one night when Ummah was pregnant with me, she dreamed a persimmon was growing in her belly. It wasn't the soft kind that bruises like a tomato, but the hard kind that is less red and more orange. Ummah knew it was a persimmon because of the cinnamon-clove scent coming off her skin, wafting out of her mouth when she exhaled. She sat for a while breathing out through her mouth and in through her nose just to make sure.

As a girl in Korea, Ummah'd heard about her own mother's dreams, especially when another baby was about to be born. In her own dream she recalled those of her mother. The tiger that stalked every night for a week before Ummah's brother arrived. The sweet pear, cold and white, that recurred from time to time before her sister, my imo, was born. Ummah knew her baby would be a girl because she dreamed of spicy-sweet persimmon.

In Ummah's dream, the fruit was a rock inside her womb, expanding by the minute, stretching her skin until she felt as if she was on fire. Ummah looked around for oil that could be massaged into her skin so that her body would go back to normal once she pushed the persimmon out. When she walked, the fruit pulled her belly downward, anchoring her to the ground, making her swing its weight from left to right, eventually making her crawl on all fours.

She lay on her back when it grew to be the size of a boulder and the sweet-spicy aroma became so thick that it formed a dense brownish cloud around her. Ummah thought the weight of the persimmon was going to kill her. She felt her kidneys exploding, her bladder being crushed underneath. Water and pulp started to rush out from between her legs, and when she reached down, she grabbed on to something hard and realized it was a slippery brown seed, as large as the palm of her hand. She held it too tight and it shot out of her grasp. It grew legs and, like a giant insect, skittered off.

The cinnamon cloud was humid. It made Ummah's hair stick to her face, to her neck. The hard persimmon started shaking inside her, impatient to emerge, as if it was suffocating or drowning. She pushed hard, instinctually, and with every muscle in her body. Her teeth exploded, one by one, until her mouth was filled with gravel and bone and ash. Her fingers were clawing at the ground beneath her until finally Ummah's body split open and a jolt of coldness sat her upright.

On the ground between her knees, the massive fruit gleamed in its pulpy afterbirth. Pebbles were stuck to the bottom and its spicy scent was mixed with a metallic bitterness that made Ummah wince just a little bit. She steadied herself and reached for it, but right where her fingers touched the sticky skin, tiny holes erupted. Her persimmon started to deflate, the air whistling quietly at first and then more loudly. Desperately, she grabbed it with both hands, but this caused it to fall into itself, melting and becoming an empty sack of slippery, rubbery skin. It hung from her fingertips and Ummah looked around to see if anyone had seen what happened, if anyone could help. No one had so no one did.

She stayed as long as she could. But one day, while I was working at the bar, Bora filled her suitcase with as much as would fit. She left traces behind in every corner of the front bedroom of our Sherbrooke and Papineau walk-up. Years later, when she returned to Canada, we half-heartedly argued over who was the rightful owner of the yellow sweater she hadn't had space for in her luggage. I wore it to paint a room. *The sleeves are too short for you anyhow*, my sister noticed.

At the airport, I cried openly but without noise. My sister tried to laugh with me. I made her uncomfortable. Bora asked, *why? I'll see you soon!* and patted my back when I tried to hold on to her for one minute more. She wished she could be everything I needed her to be. But it was too much for one person to carry. Bora wanted to go home. She didn't cry then, but said later that she hoped I hadn't taken it the wrong way. *I hardly ever cry, especially in front of my family*, she said.

Bora was exhausted. She almost missed her flight because everything was written in French and she had spent months studying English. She only knew bonjour and merci and tartine. She was afraid to ask for help in English. On the plane, she was in the centre of a row of five seats. The man sitting directly in front of her immediately reclined his chair and she could smell his unwashed hair. The journey to Narita took fifteen hours and thirteen minutes. Then one more flight before arriving home.

Maybe it was because she was nervous or maybe it was because we'd left for the airport around five in the morning, but Bora fell asleep immediately upon boarding. She felt the hum of the plane's engine, a gentle cradle. She heard the soft white noise of other passengers, a lullaby. She thought she'd slept for hours, but when she woke up, they'd not yet started to taxi back from the gate. The flight attendants were doing the safety demonstration in French. She wondered if they had already done it in English. The crew played an audio recording in Japanese, but by then they'd given up their routine and were slamming shut over-stuffed storage bins. Recalling this years later, seated at my kitchen table in Winnipeg, Bora said, *I'm sorry I had to leave the way I did. I know you were afraid we'd lose each other. But we're sisters. So I'll always come back.* She told me that as the plane took off, without anyone to witness, she started to cry.

I talk about it every so often. Whisper into the night that I am tired. Tired of feeling hurt and broken. Tired of feeling rotten. But I'm afraid of dying. When I was a child, I wished it with every birthday candle, on every star. I dreamed in death I would be reunited with my Korean mother as my Christian nanny had promised. But still today I am alive and so is Ummah, and so my wish takes on a different shade. It's not the pain of dying that scares me. It's being alone. Of being untethered to the people I've finally found. The Sunday school teachers always said that when people die, they reunite with dead family and friends. Somehow, even without their bodies, people recognize each other. Find each other. But how will I find my Korean family in death when even in life we hardly knew each other? What name will we call out in any possible afterworld? Will they even think to look for me? To find me? Or will it be my responsibility again? When I am on my cloud, how will they hold on to me? And me them?

There was a baby before me. There was a baby who died at the orphanage or agency or foster home. I only learned about her in 2009—that first time back in Korea. I was sent in her place. It would not have looked good to go back on a promise. No one could tell. There is no formula to the matching. The contracts were already signed. Was I given her birthdate, her photograph, her future?

The folder at the adoption agency in Seoul was thicker than I thought it would be. I read my Canadian parents' application. I read the home studies and racial preferences. I know what they wanted. I know what they didn't want. I know everything. I read the stories social workers made up about all of my families, skeptical that errors were only flaws in translation. I read about So Young, the baby who died. The baby I became. I want to say her name a thousand times. I want to say it every day. Because she died a whisper, an inconvenience in the transaction.

The baby has a very sweet and charming personality. She laughs constantly and is a good eater. We estimate her birthdate as early spring 1981. While her parentage is unknown, it is this social worker's opinion that she must have come from a very well-off family because her eyes are bright and responsive and the clothes she was wearing when she first came to the agency looked new. Her favourite snack is the juice of an apple. While she does not like to sleep alone, after a few minutes of crying she settles and sleeps through the night. She is approximately six months old at the time that this document was written. She bonds well with her caretakers and should have no problems attaching to adoptive parents. It should be noted that she often sleeps on her stomach, but this should not be a deterrent for adoptive parents as this behaviour can be fixed. She has a mole on her left shoulder and discoloration on her lower back, as is common of Korean babies. Please be assured that this will fade away in time. It is this worker's opinion that this baby is a good candidate for overseas adoption. She has no one in Korea.

So Young. Her name means beauty and eternity. She was only a baby when she was completely erased. No one thinks about her. No one remembers her. My Canadian parents promised me no one told them what happened to her. But they also told me it was God's plan. It was fate. Fate that So Young died and the agency sent me instead. But I can't let that settle. It cannot be fate that a baby had to die for me to become. She lives inside me because the effects of her short life impact me more than anyone else's ever have. I keep living so that I don't disappoint her, that baby no one thinks about.

At a certain point my Canadian family stopped asking. They told themselves that I was concentrating on my career, but they were curious, of course, if something was wrong. Something must have been wrong. My younger sister, their biological child, already had a daughter. They struggled to bite their tongues, indignant at first, when I didn't want to hold her baby, when I felt she wasn't mine to hold.

It wasn't my sister's baby in particular that was the problem. It was all infants and the ways people pointed out how aware they are of their lives, of their surroundings and families. How quickly they bond. How attached they are to familiar things. I'd stare blankly at their faces when they said things like that. When they'd think it was reassuring to tell me, *she recognizes you as her aunt. She knows who you are*, even though I'd only met her once.

Wasn't it obvious, then, that I too, as a baby, would have recognized and loved and found comfort in the smell of the ocean? In the sound of the city and the language around me? In the black hair and black eyes of the person or people who taught me how to say *ummah*?

I have no words to answer when people ask for donations or acknowledgement when they adopt endangered species, a stray cat or dog, a tree, a piece of highway. When well-intentioned friends wonder, *do you not want to pass down your genes?* When a salesperson tells me I should definitely have children with my spouse because, although Asiatic genes are strong, the baby will have big eyes—which is to say, improved eyes. When my Canadian family asks me, *don't you want to see your face repeated in a child's?*

Inside my long-expired Korean passport is a black-and-white photo of a six-month-old infant looking off to the left. Paint flecks the colour of rust peel off and stick to fingers when the brittle cover is handled. The documents are worn not from use but from age. My Korean passport smells like a library book. Like a church basement. The characteristics listed on the personal information page mean nothing. Hair: Black. Eyes: Black. Height: 62.5 cm. Really, it could be anyone in that photo. If you flip the page, there is a place to list accompanying minors. I wonder about the government employee at the passport office, processing this document for a baby when the biometric records are obviously imagined for an adult—someone old enough to be travelling with children of their own. Almost all of the pages are empty. At the very back are a number of stickers, proving that someone paid the proper people the proper fees. There is a letter stapled inside, midway through the book. It reminds the document holder that her Korean passport, alongside any claim to citizenship, expires in six months. My Korean passport was disposable: issued for a single purpose, a one-time-only use.

I came to Canada with five months left on my passport, one toy in my hand, and one word in my mouth. They must have misheard me, because they tell me now that I was crying *um-mama*, unable or unwilling to let me believe I had something that wasn't vaguely recognizable to a Western listener. But I know I was calling out *ummah*. That early on, I was a Korean girl. They laughed at the noise I made because to them it meant nothing. But to me, it was all there ever was.

Before I arrived, my parents had a name picked out, but when they saw me, they decided it wasn't a good fit. So they changed it at the last moment. Gave my sister, born a few months after I arrived, the name they'd planned for me. I became one of many girls at school called the same thing. We were all identified by our shared given name and one more initial that separated us or, in the case where two or more girls had family names that started with the same letter, the whole thing. It wasn't until I was dreaming of names for the children I thought I might have that I pondered how odd it was to think that a girl like me, with my eyes and hair and skin, would fit one English name better than any other. How out of place I must have seemed lined up with all the other Jennys, as if an initial was needed to tell me apart from the rest of them.

It happened every so often, but one time in particular stands out in my mind. Our family ate supper each night around a small table in the kitchen, not in the dining room, which was for special occasions only. For whatever reason, my name was the topic of conversation. My Korean name had been reserved as a third and fourth name. My parents didn't know that a Korean given name has two syllables. On all my government documents, my Korean name is split in two. We all mispronounced it for years. That night from my memory, at the kitchen table, my parents sing-songed, *hei yun, hi yun, ho yun*, and then my sister did the same. They sounded like my schoolmates when they mocked *Ching Chong Chang*, and I knew that I was a joke and my name was a joke too.

Years later, we practised saying it together. The rising first syllable, the dreamy second, blurred together like a sigh. My rhythm grew increasingly stilted, slower. My name broken into two distinct syllables again, instead of the beautiful combination. Her voice became more frustrated each time. Me, then her. Me, then her. *We were told your name was pronounced differently from what you're saying.* She's consistent with that memory that dismisses my knowledge of my own name, my Korean family members' voices as they say it. I try to trace out the letters, but only one of us knows the alphabet. I don't remember who was first to give up trying, my Canadian mother or me.

Unni . . . How much do you think we would have shared if we'd been raised together? They probably would have told people we were twins. Of course, your mother would have treated me differently. That makes sense. Anyhow, I would've wanted to live with my own mother. So I guess even if I hadn't been sent to Canada, we'd still be strangers. I have a sister in Canada, right? We're almost the same age too. When we were little, shopkeepers used to call us "the twins." My parents laughed and I understood, at too young an age, why it was so funny. That I was the joke.

Can you imagine, unni, never having seen Korean people when you were young? I think that's why I hated myself at different points in my childhood. Of course that's why. But then, when I did meet Koreans in college, most of them laughed at me too, because I couldn't understand anything they were saying.

Unni . . . I don't think I know what your laugh sounds like. I've memorized your smile, but have I ever heard you laugh? Maybe you don't feel like it. Maybe there's nothing to laugh about.

They tell me I was a happy child. *What happened?* they ask, even though they know the answer, and if they don't, they wouldn't like what I have to say anyhow. My Canadian mother recalls often that when I first arrived, I stayed awake through the night. *Babies do that*, people told her. But not all babies have jet lag.

I'm told that one time, early on, something broke through that layer of happiness. I was a toddler in the back seat of the family car. It was a day trip. Suddenly I shattered and only stopped sobbing when I was slapped across the face. *Lightly*, she promises, demonstrating on me now nearly every time we meet. Still, I flinch at being touched. *We didn't know how to stop you*, they say. *We didn't know what was wrong.*

I turned another year older. On paper, that is—because no one really knows how accurate those documents are after all. Today, I refuse to believe in any of those things. But on my sixth birthday I had a party. At the party, I asked my parents if they believed my Korean mother thought of me, at least, when that one day rolled around each year. Many years later they admitted that, until then, they hadn't realized I ever thought about her. *Of course I did*, I told them, emboldened by having finally found the words. By having finally found the people who help me practise those words.

The students in my first-grade French class called her Mademoiselle R., because no one could pronounce her family name. Now I recognize in her name the world from where her recent ancestors must have come. I recognize what must be carved into one of the thicker branches of her family tree.

She was so beautiful and I was in love with her. We were what someone, years later, described to me as kinfolk, yet racial strangers. As a six-year-old, I told a schoolmate that Mademoiselle R. was my mother. My friend was generous enough to ignore me and my delusions. Or maybe to them, colour was colour. I knew we weren't the same. I also understood we were together in our difference from everyone else.

On very special days, Mademoiselle R. would hold my hand and we'd walk around the schoolyard. Once, I tripped and my mouth and elbow began to bleed. Mademoiselle R. knelt down and held on to me, and then she peered straight into my face. Her eyes, like mine, were black. Maybe the blackest I'd ever seen. I saw myself in her eyes.

It could have been the hours perched on a piano bench, but probably it was that other thing that set my back so stiff as a girl. Today, my spine arches and twists and cups forward. The look of a woman ready to be leaned into. But back then, I was so hard. I stood at attention, stiffened by the threat of that word the boy called me to make his friends laugh at my reddened face. When my only answer through the mortification of it all was what my parents urged me to reply: *I'm not even Chinese.*

When I was six, I had my first operation. It was cosmetic, or that's what they would call it nowadays; in 1987 it was still plastic surgery. Elected. The decision was made to pin back one ear that tilted slightly outwards. I know now that it was possibly genetic, though I've not thought to ask other Korean family members if they had the same condition, but I used to imagine my protruding ear was evidence of my mother's labour, her body clenched around me one last time, wanting to hold me in. Wanting to hold me inside her forever.

I had a cast around my head all summer. That was the year I stopped swimming lessons. Leading up to my operation, nurses took blood. *Just in case*, they said mysteriously. I didn't mind watching the needle go in, the blood come out. And I was brave up until the moment when I was in a hospital bed, waiting in the hallway. I was alone then. They put a beige oxygen mask over my face. It smelled like rubber. I thought I'd sat upright screaming, and when I woke up after, I was afraid I'd be in trouble. I hadn't, so I wasn't. I have very few memories of my childhood, but I do remember that day. I remember the balloons in my recovery room. And I remember the doll my mother placed on my chest as I was wheeled out of the pre-op room. I cried onto that doll when I was in the hallway waiting, afraid. She'd been a Christmas gift the year before. A baby doll with short black hair and a plastic face. *It looks like you,* my parents told me when I unwrapped her. The day of the operation, I cried down onto her hard white face and blue, never-blinking eyes.

I was seven years old when first I became a Korean girl in the eyes of those around me. It was 1988 and the Olympics were hosted in Seoul. I became a Korean girl at that moment, because up until then I had been an unidentified Asian who laughed along when someone pulled their eyes back and said *chop suey* or *chicken chow mein* with a certain tone in their voice. The meanness wasn't directed at me. My friends may not have noticed I was there, or maybe they thought of me as one of them. I laughed out of confusion, but also out of fear. I laughed not because I thought it was funny but because it seemed like the safest way to disappear.

To the other children at school and my teachers, who trusted post-racial mottoes that we're all the same, I transformed into a Korean girl overnight. Then, all of a sudden, I had to answer for a country and culture I'd never known. My peers sing-songed nonsense words they thought they'd heard on the news. I laughed. Some of the more outgoing boys offered fake-out martial-art chops and leapt crane kicks. I laughed some more, though I didn't catch the reference. One teacher asked me to defend Korean dog-eating, which was the first time I'd heard of that. The students were horrified. They called me a dog-eater, which was neither original nor the last time I would hear it. I had nothing to say. So I laughed. And became a Korean girl once again.

Ummah, that time at Chuseok, when you took me to the park behind the school in Gimcheon where you studied as a girl and sat me on a swing, when you gave me a tentative push—did you feel the full weight of my adult body, or did I seem lighter than that? Was I the daughter of your dreams —the one you'd tried to erase from your mind—or was I someone new? Did you see my blond hair streaming behind, or were there two nearly-black plaits rocking back and forth, tied unevenly with ribbons? Could you hear the happy-scared giggle? The whistle of a lisp from behind a loose front tooth? The excited panic when you realize your legs are too short to touch the ground and put on the brakes?

Over the years, I've tried to piece together the splintered story of my sister's life with our mother when Bora was young. But what is a life when all the stories come out of order and many, I can tell, are hidden still? What is a story when the speaker and the listener live in different languages? When neither is certain that love and kinship are unconditional?

I think my mother's husband was cruel. Bora tells me she wishes he, her father, was dead. She tells me Ummah hated him so much she'd leave in the night, sacrificing her two remaining children so she could be free. She'd always return, push-pulled by love and hatred. Or fear for herself and fear for her children. Bora tells me this as fact.

Imo told me that before I reappeared in 2009, before she learned that my father's father had sent me away, she thought I was dead. She said my mother married a man and hoped she could trust him to protect the small memory she had of me and not turn me into something ugly. Imo mimed his drunkenness. When I fact-checked with my sister, Bora said he also gambled. She said, *I have no father.*

Ummah told me her husband threatened to open her up in front of the world, unearth me. I became a bullet aimed at her heart each time he lost his job or the odds were against him. She paid. My grandparents paid. Probably my eldest uncle paid to keep me buried.

Bora didn't know. When it was happening, Imo didn't know. Neither of them knew the entire story when they began living together. My sister was fourteen at the time. When Bora returned home to Seoul a year later, her father was gone. Our brother too, from what I understand, was gone.

Once, we were on a flight from Florida. I was eight. The flight attendant asked me where I was from, and I told her South Korea. She laughed. My parents laughed. Everyone laughed, because she meant to ask where I was flying home to that day, what was the final destination after our connection. Two things: I was so accustomed to strangers asking me where I was from that I parroted personal information without thinking. And second, I had to teach myself, when I was grown, to refuse to answer that question depending on who was asking. I had to learn that being visible isn't the same thing as being seen. Really being seen.

Unni . . . Did you know that when I was small I sometimes hated myself so deeply that I imagined death, but in that dream my face-down eight-year-old body, washed up in the weeds of the riverbank, had freckled arms and strawberry-blond hair, straight and thin? When you look at me with your head tilted to the left, your eyes softening, as though you pity me, it makes me think that you can sense the sorrow that fills my mouth with stones, stopping me from speaking, breathing.

If you could be any kind of Asian, what would you choose?
I asked my mother one day when I was in middle school.
She was driving. I was in the passenger seat, watching
my reflection in the side mirror the way I always did.
Japanese, she said, after a quick moment of consideration.

When I was first in Korea, on the train from Daegu to Gimcheon, it occurred to me that my grandparents in Canada also came from a place with soil so rich that the tender, curling fingers of grapevines wrapped themselves around the antique trunks of their neighbours. The grapes of my childhood were different from those of my birth, those of my ancestors. Smaller and grown mostly for wine. But my grandparents from each family, the ones who planted and tended and juiced and sold the grapes, and the ones who drank it as wine just four times a year, and even then only when paired with the body of Christ, are now buried near the vineyards in the soft black dirt that made their yields so full.

On car trips to visit my Canadian grandparents, I'd stare out the window silently. But really, I was watching the curve of my eyelid, barely perceptible in the daylight reflection.

Years later, I noticed someone I loved very much watching himself in the mirror when he thought no one was looking. *Why do you do that?* I asked, seeking explanation for why I couldn't stay away from my own reflection. He answered: *It's the only way I know I exist.*

When I entered middle school, the years began to flicker together. The world saw me differently the more I had to stand alone as an adolescent Korean girl because without my parents on either side, my proximate whiteness dissolved away. I was launched into Asian womanhood by myself. My hands were empty. My heart was not ready. There was no one to explain how grown men would look at me. Touch me. The ways they saw me that were different from the other girls in my class. The storylines they loved. The pornography they watched. There was no one to forgive me for the ways I sought approval or to name aloud some of the reasons I offered myself up in the ways I did. There was just my shame. Being opened, a Butterfly, pinned through the heart with my wings spread. I felt, at the time, it was a fair exchange just to be wanted for what I thought were good reasons and not for bad.

Unni . . . Did I tell you about the first boy I kissed and the way he called me on the phone a few days later? I overheard him describe me and then protest after a friend said, I bet she looks like this. Can you imagine, unni, how my heart started to race, how I held my breath, imagining bucked teeth and pulled-back eyes? It didn't surprise me when, at school a few days later, I heard rumours that I was dumped. What would you have said, unni, after my heart was broken for the first time? You would have been too busy with your own middle-school life. But maybe you would have brushed my bangs out of my face, or given me some banana milk. Or maybe you would have walked up to him and told him to fuck right off as soon as the news reached you. Yeah, that's it.

Would you have warned me, unni, that the forty-year-old ski-lift operator or that high school teacher had no business talking to me the ways they did? That I shouldn't have let them touch me like that? Would you have told our father? Would he have cared? Did I tell you that one boyfriend hit me so hard, my jaw has clicked and ached ever since? I definitely didn't tell you about that college affair with a woman who would stroke my stomach and tell me she loved how juvenile my body looked, or my first serious girlfriend whose father called me a China doll and asked, how's the rice? each time we met. I understand you've also had some bad relationships. I wonder if, when we were children, I would have listened in on your phone calls and read your diaries, and then told your secrets not because I was bad but because I was protective and jealous. I wonder if, when we became young women, we would have confessed all these things to each other.

The comments, glances, when I was with my Canadian father started when I was a teenager. He loves me. But around that time I had to lean back because of how strangers saw us. I was twelve when, at a hardware store, the clerk asked if the rakes we were buying were *his and hers*. White women averted their gaze, but I could hear them sucking the back of their teeth with their dangerous tongues. White men stared with what I can, at best, only interpret as curiosity, but always they watched without shame.

Those glances travelled with me into adulthood, and when it came time to plan my marriage, I'm sorry to admit, I let them take me over. I know I hurt my father by refusing to walk down the church aisle with him. What he doesn't know is that the reason there was no music, no dancing, is that I was afraid of that tradition too. I hope one day he forgives me. I hope he understands.

I was raised in a small town with a large German-Canadian community. The town was originally called Berlin, but that was replaced by the name of a notorious British imperialist. My high school boyfriend's parents, I learned years later, disapproved of me for all the most predictable reasons. His cousin once said I wasn't good enough to hang around her family. Another boyfriend's house featured a painting of his dead grandfather in their living room. The two lightning bolt *S*'s were prominent on the collar of his military uniform. That same boyfriend had childhood friends who warned him about me. *She seems sneaky*, they said, and he thought it was no big deal to tell me.

I ate schnitzel with my uncle on Thursday nights at a restaurant called the Eidelweiss. As a girl, I waved at Uncle Hans in the parade. I'm convinced that my skill at kimchi comes in part from my familiarity with sauerkraut. And once, when I was in my late teens, my mother suggested I audition to be Miss Oktoberfest. I remember having no response. It wasn't because I was opposed to pageants. And it wasn't because I thought those girls were more beautiful than me. But to put things into perspective, look through any of the archives that feature photographs of the young women who've been crowned with this honour. It seems obvious why that contest, and really that town, wasn't for me.

⁓⟨

The nails of my middle fingers moved as if by their own design to dig into the cuticles on my inner thumbs. Skin all around was raw and jagged. I'd pry it up and then scratch it off, sometimes switching to use my index fingers like chisels, planes, peeling back layer after layer. I stopped mutilating my hands a few years ago, when I was in my mid-thirties. Before that, all of my fingers were damaged down to the first knuckle. Always at some stage of healing. Bandages rotated from one finger to another. I'd done it since elementary school. It hurt, but I couldn't stop peeling off my skin. Tearing off my fingerprints.

Why do they think their love is so good that it is all we'll ever need? How can anyone's love be *that* good?

Early on, in the first days of her living with us in Montreal, I warned Bora in the fractured English I used when we talked, mirroring her because somehow that felt more understandable, that men in the West would see her differently than men in Korea did. She'd come to understand, through experience, what I tried to explain. Back then, because it was her first time away from Korea, I worried. I remembered her insistence that I not take taxis in Seoul. This time, it was me who struggled to find the words to explain *exotic* or *ornament* or *fetish*. I had no words for *submissive*. No words to summarize the violence of *Madame Butterfly*. *Miss Saigon*. No words to explain *tight 18yo Oriental slut begging for it*.

When high school ended, I moved immediately to Toronto for my studies. My first friend was a white woman. It is through her that I met other people of colour: The Chinese Canadian student with whom my professors continually confused me. The Black woman who taught me how to crochet. The Filipino guy who commuted an hour and a half each day. How they saw me, I can't imagine. In that multicultural space, amongst people already so sure of themselves, I was learning to be a woman of colour. With them, but still so aware that I was alone.

I met a Korean Canadian woman in my third year of university. She was beautiful. She taught me liquid eyeliner. She taught me how to say *I love you* in the language she spoke with her parents. Sometime later, I thought back to my friendship with her when I first said *sarang he-yo* to my Korean mother. I'd been practising that phrase all those years.

The first time I tasted Korea, I was twenty and alone. It was 2001 and I took the subway to Christie station in Toronto one late fall evening. I wasn't dressed for the weather. Just outside the station was a dark restaurant, empty except for a few lonely college students who didn't look up from their engineering textbooks splattered with rusty soup stains. The table smelled like bleach and a mouldy kitchen cloth that hadn't been wrung out enough the day before. The menu, laminated plastic, was sticky and smelled the same.

An older woman, someone I now know might be called *ajumma* by a cheekily familiar diner or *sun seng nim* by a more respectful and cautious one, brought an entire jug of water and an empty plastic cup. She spoke quickly in Korean before turning and leaving. I wondered if she assumed I was one of the homesick international students who trekked twenty minutes from U of T to settle their bodies the way only certain foods can. I scanned the menu, trying to choose by photograph instead of name. The woman returned. Spoke again, and realized I could not understand. She asked in carefully selected nouns and verbs if I'd been born in Canada. If my parents had been born in Canada.

I had no words then, even fewer than I have now. I mimed rocking a baby. Then the wings of an airplane with both arms awkwardly splayed. I pointed to my closed mouth and shook my head. She seemed to understand, because she let out a sigh, a sympathetic *aigo*, and turned and walked into the kitchen. Just as I was thinking it had been a mistake to come to K-town by myself, she returned with a sizzling rock bowl. She placed it in front of me. *Spicy?* she asked. I nodded, wanting to experience what I'd read was the fiery heat of Korean food.

Red sauce was squirted from a plastic bottle, the sort that holds ketchup in diners that serve crinkle-cut french fries and grilled cheese sandwiches made with white bread and Kraft slices. The woman took a long silver spoon from a box on the table. I hadn't noticed it there before. She made chopping motions, cutting through the vegetables, meat, and egg displayed in the bowl like a sun and its rays. She chopped and stirred, and the bowl hissed. A layer of rice was revealed. It quickly turned red as everything, including what I'd later know to be the earthy red pepper paste gochujang, was stirred in. She pressed some of the food onto the spoon and handed it to me. Without speaking, I took it and ate, even though I'd been a vegetarian for years already. I felt my skin vibrate from the spice. My tongue recoiled from the heat. The woman, who was neither my mother nor my grandmother, neither my sister nor my aunt, placed her hand on my shoulder for a moment as I tasted creamy, charred, bitter, and sweet Korea.

⸙

Sometimes, still, I feel so completely unmoved by hunger that I wonder how long I can go without eating. I dare myself to let the hollow feeling where my throat meets my chest settle there. One day? Two? I think about the hundreds of wasted sandwiches that I hid in the corners of desks, bottoms of lockers, rotting because I could never bring myself to eat in front of others. I remember my Canadian parents' jokes about how I would hide food when I first arrived as a baby. How I had a one-track mind. How I once stole a radish at the grocery store when I was small enough to sit in the cart and my mother insisted I confess my sins to the produce manager, who couldn't have cared less. But I remember the shame. Then there are the years I spent starving myself in college, the illusion of control, or throwing up the rottenness I thought had found its way in. The ways even today that anxiety triggers days of starvation, especially when I'm away from home. How I attend work conferences prepared with sugar packets and electrolytes, avoid large gatherings where I might need to eat in front of others. Or not eat and then be questioned about that. I think about how the noises bodies emit when they are suffering for food make the corners of my lips curl in smug superiority.

Once, when I was in my early twenties, my Canadian parents gifted me a book of letters by Korean birth mothers. I read that book alone in my old bedroom, unchanged since I'd left home. I was afraid of the letters. Trying to see myself in them and imagining one of the authors my mother.

I had lovers in my twenties who tried to solve me.
Dark-eyed and dark-haired and dark-skinned lovers who
wanted the idea of me, and I of them. One man said,
twisting my hair around his fingertips, *I would never use
that word*. He said, *I would never call you a bitch*. He said,
*you're beautiful like all the others, but you're beautiful on the
inside too*. When he was away, he said, *I miss your touch,
your taste, your spirit lying next to me*. But then he said,
*you need to make the most of it or you're not evolving fast
enough*. He said, *your anger makes me angry. Your sadness
makes me angry*. Then he said, *you're not worthy of being
the mother of my children because you're damaged goods*.
He said, *you're a fraud because you look like a woman I'd
want to put children inside of, but you're rotten at your core*.

She didn't stay in Korea long once she left Montreal. Maybe, like me, she came to realize there was little for her there. For different reasons, of course. Bora'd hinted at the impossibility of living in Korea for young women like her, without wealth or social standing. I'd witnessed people working themselves to death. I read an article once that said South Korea's population was at risk because young people couldn't afford to have families. The article also noted that some Koreans regretted sending so many children overseas for adoption because now the future of the nation was unstable. The population was depleting at a frightening rate.

So she left soon after her return. I'm not sure where she went first, because we lost track of each other for a handful of years. But then I saw photos of her on social media. Once she posed in front of the Taj Mahal. Once she was in the Australian outback. Once in a classroom in the Philippines. Once hiking in the mountains of Nepal. All that time, we didn't speak. But I knew that she was out in the world somewhere.

Try for me, little sister, to stand up and dare them all to maintain eye contact.

Bora—dongseng—as the word troisième *fades from your neck with each visit to the laser tattoo remover, I know it is not me whom you erase but the error that we ever thought of you as last. Third-born, second to leave, but first to riot against the land that made it so easy for them to dismiss us. To dismiss our mother.*

I can't imagine you as a little girl, my little girl, because you never were. To me, you were born a twenty-something woman. But you are my woman and I am yours.

I ached when I learned, weeks too late, that after you returned to Korea from Montreal, you travelled to the mountains of Nepal and that, while there, the ground trembled and cracked and broke open. I want there to be a genetic string that tethers us so I can feel your fear and anger and joy across the hemispheres.

I see in your many migrations an anger towards those who made you think home was important and then not. I feel it too. I watch you age in the pictures that stream at me online. You are so lovely.

I never saw myself here. Where sky goes on forever. And francophones pass undetected like the best secret agents. We came to Winnipeg the same year Bora went home to Korea. There was no Montreal without her. Driving across northern Ontario, the Canadian Shield, the evergreens, the quiet—it all reminded me of Gimcheon. The place I knew my Korean parents returned to as the site to regrow their love. We'd not spoken, my parents and I, since the days following my marriage, and I couldn't imagine just the two of them alone. But they'd chosen a place from the past to try to make something new. I wondered if they thought of me sometimes and how I'd been growing in my mother's body in that very town.

For a short while in 2012, I knew an American man who was older than me by many years. He'd never met another Korean adoptee before. Not face to face, at least. He wanted to search for his Korean family. I told him about my life. He wanted to talk about feeling left out, how we'd never fully belong anywhere. I told him even more. I watched for that moment when he realized we're the same. That as misfits, we fit together. That same feeling coursed through me back in 2008 when first I met other adoptees like me. I fell in love with one of them. Quietly, of course. And in the way people who fall in love with those similar are actually learning to love themselves. Through him, that man from 2008, I learned about birth searches. I met others like us. I met others through him. I wanted to introduce that new American man to other people too. To make him feel connected. But before I could, I received a phone call from his wife, who warned me to stay away.

Unni . . . I need to talk to you about a man. A man whom I think about every day. A beautiful man who flew into the night when at last he said, enough. Because under the care of a leader who promised change, who promised hope spray-painted red and white and black and blue, he was ripped from the only country he knew and returned, a factory defect from the assembly line that promises butterfly kisses and violin prodigies. Undocumented, inconvenient, he was no longer the gwiyeobda ticket to Protestant Heaven. He was no longer Babylift-baby gift-that-keeps-on-giving. He grew into a man. A beautiful Korean man. A beautiful interrupted Korean man who came to the United States as an eight-year-old boy. Whose white parents branded him with their name and thought that was all there was to it. Deported, unregistered, stateless, homeless, wordless. Unni . . . were you working your shift at Incheon International the day this beautiful interrupted Korean man landed in a country that not only had forgotten him but had sold him thirty years earlier? There are many people like him in Seoul, in Busan, in Daegu, all over. They're washing your dishes and cleaning your homes and doing any other job where they don't have to speak. So they don't have to interact with the people who'd rather forget that seventy years after the fighting has stopped, Korea still exports children at thousands of dollars a pop. Did you hear about this beautiful interrupted Korean man, unni, in the news when his ashes arrived back in Pennsylvania and they announced that, in death, he

*finally came to the U.S. legally? You know they send us over,
they send us around the world, infants alone on airplanes,
ashes labelled cargo, mail order our entire lives. Did you
think of me, made of papers forged to close the sale, without
family registry, without birth certificate or accurate
passport? Did you know, unni?*

My question is, *why?* But I know there is no answer. At least not to me. Colonialism. White saviourhood. Orientalism. Impatience. Far-away birth mothers. No take-backs. *Which is it?*

Artist unknown. (Korean, Jeolla Province, Life dates unknown.) Ham (wedding box), late 1800/early 1900s, wood, nickel fittings, lacquer finish.

Listen patiently and you can hear the chatter of bored work-study students making plans for the weekend before fall classes start. You can also hear the artificial clicking of the keyboard on my phone, hasty and staccato. Instead, I want to hear the hinges creaking and the locks snapping open, fingers clawing treasures into crevices of a bridal hanbok worn once not too long ago—a key swallowed in vain because they're coming with axes. But they keep it shut, two feet away from me and behind a velvet rope, so I can't reach out and stroke the buckles without notice. I imagine soldiers scrounging, finding flimsy savings, jeering at their meagreness but snatching them away anyhow. I imagine postwar professors travelling abroad and *tsk*ing in sympathy for the poor bastards who had to sell their family heirlooms. Those same professors finger the rounded corners of my great-grandmother's bridal trunk, imagining it in their home study and one day in a gallery where theirs will be the only known name. I see the collector bartering, already anticipating how he'll re-enact the deal at dinner parties for the next ten years, regaling guests with his knowledge of Korean culture, his eye for the most exquisite antiques. They'll be thoroughly entertained. They'll admire the craftsmanship, pity the poor, and pass the salt.

Gangnam-gu is more than a centre of luxury, infinite skyscrapers glinting fish cresting in formation. More than overpriced fusion ddeokbokki, than a handbag museum shaped like the vintage tote I inherited from my Canadian mother. It's more than a vaguely recognizable string of syllables in the song by that pop artist who was way more interesting than he was given credit for. It is where a guesthouse attached to an adoption agency, my adoption agency, hosts returned adoptees alongside people who've travelled to Korea to pick up new children. Where agency workers pretend to take responsibility, in the form of affordable housing, for the sorrow they have profited from, while forcing us to reckon with the fact that it's still going on. They're sorry, but only a little bit. Fifty dollars a night, which is a hundred less than a hotel room. That's how sorry they are. A hundred discounted U.S. dollars of sorry. I never stayed there, but I came across a summary of this place online. A blogger described living at the guesthouse as their adoption paperwork was being completed. The review was from 2014. They were there for a baby. As though lying in wait, they described the agency and how they caught a glimpse of women who'd not yet given birth.

I was wearing, again, the silk dress Ummah bought me in Seoul. I wear it all the time. I wear it with my hair pulled back because the collar comes up to my throat. The fabric is pilled on both sides, where my arms brush against the dress. I was speaking to an auditorium of students celebrating Asian Heritage Month in Winnipeg. I admitted that sometimes I feel I have no heritage. I explained that my increasingly threadbare dress was the closest thing to heritage I had. That the fact that I became a teacher, a reader, of Asian North American literature made sense. It was one of the only ways I could access the spaces and people I'd been denied.

The audience asked questions. The students were shy, but their teachers were not. A white man in the back row went first. *Why did your mother abandon you?* he thought he had the right to know. In that moment, my hair, the dress, everything was too tight.

I sleep with the palms of my hands together, fingers aligned the way Sunday school teachers taught us was most pious when we'd chant, *I pray the Lord my soul to take*. I sleep with them pressed underneath my husband's body. His rib cage. His hip. Sometimes his head. I sleep like that so I am anchored down, tethered. So that I don't float away in the night. I sleep like that so I know where I'll be if I awake the next day.

3.

같이. GahtChi.

Together.

In my dreams, Ummah travels to the flat white fields of my Canadian home to find me. Her hair is long again, not permed so tightly to hide that it's thinning on top. It's winter and she's walking on the snow-covered Assiniboine River, the ice underneath nearly a foot thick. She just follows the path of the river and it will lead her to my house. Even though it looks cold, even though it smells cold, Ummah feels nothing in her simple dress. Along the way she sees a space cleared off and boarded in a rectangle. A bench is set up so that children can tie on their ice skates. She keeps her eyes down because the sun is so bright and she has to avoid the frozen dog shit that is just left along the way, as if there are different rules on ice than on sidewalks. Finally she arrives at the clearing and sees the steep slope she is to overcome in order to reach me. At this point in my dream, I'm there too and can see Ummah below on the river path while I wait on the ledge of the bank up above. My Korean is perfect, so I explain how to edge up the hill and grab on to the pricking branches of young trees and bushes to anchor herself. I'm calling out encouragements, and if Ummah wasn't breathing so heavily and trying to keep balance, she would compliment me on how much my language has improved. When she's nearly there, she starts to lose footing and, looking down, we both realize that she's wearing white sneakers, tractionless, of no use for climbing such a steep incline. Ummah reaches for a branch with tiny red berries all the way down. But when she grabs it, the fruit explodes in her hands and she springs back because it stings. I awaken with that last image of my mother in my mind. She's falling back down to the river, back into the snow, her hands bloody and empty and reaching.

They all came back to me—we all came back together —but everything changed. I'd grown cautious, if not skeptical, about kinship in ways I hadn't been before. First, after some distress, my relationship with my Canadian family predictably fractured. But the cracks exposed the places where repair could be made, and we found each other again and tried to move forward. Then, when grief drew me home to Korea a second time, I allowed myself to be sutured once more onto the skeleton of that family tree, recognizing how, again, fear and loss were steering my heart.

When Bora came back to me, she landed first in Vancouver and stayed there awhile. She came with the man I'd seen in photos. They met in Australia harvesting sandalwood. He told her of his long-time dream to live in Canada. She told him she had an older sister who'd been raised in that very place.

We drove to see them, my husband and I. When last she was in Canada, back in Montreal, she'd been so different. There was a whispered confidence that streamed out of her now. She smiled, showing all her teeth, when she introduced me to the man who soon would become her husband.

*Bora, dongseng . . . You'd been in Vancouver for a month,
but you didn't want to meet at your apartment. Just the way
you never invited me when we were both in Seoul. Five years
had passed since we saw each other last. I pretended I didn't
notice you sitting on the iron bench at Broadway and
Commercial. It was dusk, so it wasn't difficult to fake being
startled when you ran to me as you always do, like your shoes
are too large or your legs too skinny to lift them. It makes you
seem younger, smaller than you are.*

*Back the first time you were in Canada, in 2010, I took
you to Toronto two times and both times I showed you what
my life had been like before we even knew that the other
existed. One night on our second visit, it was so humid that,
walking past College Park, the ash from the food vendor's
grill rose up and stuck to our damp skin. I lived there, I
said, pointing at a row of windows because I couldn't
actually remember which one had been mine. I know, you
said. You told me last time. It was too grey, too busy. So
we left the next day.*

*Then, in March 2016, it was so strange to come home to
Winnipeg and see you, dongseng, in Wolseley, standing at
my front door, welcoming me into my two-and-a-half-storey
that was painted purple a few summers earlier. I was away
for a number of months and you and your boyfriend had
relocated to the Prairies in that time. You corralled the dogs.
You poured the tea. You asked me if I'd eaten and then
served me some cake on one of the chipped plates. Winnipeg*

was melting early that year and my new boots were covered in that springtime slip that oozes out when you step on waterlogged grass. You washed the dishes before I could stand up from the table. At least you let me drive when we had to go to the store.

I was away, working in California for four months, when you arrived in Winnipeg, ready to build a life, to build a family, alongside mine. We were all idealistic, but soon certain threads began to fray when your beloved lost his status, when you worked shifts so long at a sushi restaurant that your body started to break apart. But seeing photographs of you in those early moments, seeing photographs of you in my house . . . hopefulness washed down over me. Even if we all knew it would never be possible, we wanted to believe that we could live the way normal sisters live. We made a worthy effort. We tried our best. We still try our best.

It doesn't look like me, Bora said at last. I was drawing her eyebrows up instead of down. I'd never heard of anyone drawing their eyebrows down before. Maybe it was a Korean thing. But she was right—it didn't look like her even though I'd barely started. The smallest stroke of eyeliner changed her face completely. Maybe it was because her eyes are so large compared with mine. Without monolids, she doesn't need to cake the liner on the way I do.

It's okay, I told her. She didn't want to offend. But on that day it was absolutely necessary that she tell me the truth.

We'd been around the idea of truth several times before. A few months earlier we had had a phone conversation and I told her she had to quit the polite equivocating and deference. I needed to know her actual feelings and thoughts if I was going to help her move to Canada permanently.

We can't pressure them, I remember thinking back then, even though I wanted, maybe needed, the assurance that they were committed to staying. Otherwise I would start to distance myself from them, anticipating that they'd leave one day and never look back. They needed to tell me the truth and I had to be settled with their answer. Otherwise they'd never stay. She'd never stay. Let her come back on her own, I told myself. Wild birds have to come back on their own. They might wander up to you, if they think you're not looking, but if you move a muscle, they will skitter away. I commanded myself to wait for her.

Don't move, I said to myself as much as to her when I dusted her cheeks with powder, when I slipped white wildflowers into her hair and adjusted her veil.

Once, when I was in Vancouver for work, I bled onto the silk dress Ummah bought me. The unexpected blood that sometimes surprises adult women who've grown so arrogant as to think their bodies are predictable. Rhythmic. As I scratched at the stains, watching the blood distill into a hotel sink filled with cold water, I wondered at the unsuitability of my body to give life. Of my body to ever be mine.

Time and again, shame would fold down onto me—
featherlight but all-covering—to the point where I
recognized the feeling and the source while still a child.
Or it'd rush from the centre of my chest outwards.
Rhizomorphs. Up my neck. Down each limb until I was
drowned in its heat. The sex-ed documentary at the
Ontario Science Centre. The ultrasound photograph on
a pregnant friend's social media. The illustrated cross-
section of a flattened and spread-out womb at the
fertility clinic that made my head spin and the doctor
hesitate before asking if I was certain I was in the right
place. The mere suggestion that life comes from within
us—that it is all natural.

Once, I ate a peach and, while sucking the last strings of meat from the stone, felt it quiver in my mouth and split open. The inquisitive antennae of a large black beetle prodded the back of my teeth, the roof of my mouth, wondering what happened to its house. I spit it, a wad of colours, onto the ground and turned around as the beetle shimmered away from its sweet-and-sour home.

I'm afraid. I'm afraid that my insides really are rotten and that soon hairline breaks will race across my smooth granite face and people will know what's actually going on underneath. It's slippery and fermented, but also peppery and hot. I lie in my bed sometimes and while other women might lovingly caress their own breasts, their own thighs, to feel pleasure and warmth, my hands roam in search of a crack. A chink. A weakness.

You hear all the time about throwaway women. People treated like trash and eventually shucked because they're up against a world that hates their skin, their hair, their eyes, their sex, their blood, their god, their wealth, their poverty.

But I was a throwaway woman the minute I was born. They must have detected that I was rotted on the inside. A fragrant peach with a festering pit made bad by a beetle consuming it from the inside out. They must have seen something bad deep within me, because they discarded me even though I was so beautiful on the outside. Even though my hair was thick, my mouth was red, and my eyes were shining and wet.

I've cultivated this false beauty my entire life. I've worshipped it even while I've hated it. I'm scared now because lines are starting to appear where once my face was intact. These lines are just the beginning. I know that soon they'll become deeper, crevices even, carved out and

eroding. And then the rot inside me, which some saw the
minute I was born, will be exposed, clear for all to see,
for all to know.

The seed-filled pods from the ash tree into which the clothesline has been drilled and the still-wet body of a demolished ladybug fell onto my bare stomach as I lay out in the backyard one Mother's Day afternoon. The pods left tiny black dots on my skin. Elsewhere in the yard, the Japanese lilac burst forth with its funereal perfume. Nausea flooded in.

I heard somewhere that foreign relatives can be sponsored to come to Canada through a special program. Something about being a grandparent whose family lives elsewhere. The rules are always changing, but at the time, all of a sudden, I felt the drive to become a mother.

But while most people are thinking about their future when they have a child, I was still running after my past. Wanting to become a parent so that I might be my mother's child again. Thinking that my mother would come to me and show me how to be both.

Three times a week I'd lie down on the examination table, the strip of paper down the centre crackling as I tried not to tear it at the start of the appointment. The room had a certain smell, but it wasn't the alcohol that was sealed in a glass flute and in which a pair of medical scissors were submerged up to their hinge. It wasn't incense or herbs or anything that might make someone cough. Each time, at eleven-thirty, the aroma of Chinese soup, the kind with chunks of beef on the bottom and peas and sesame oil spots floating on top, wafted into the three tiny rooms.

When the doctor shuffled in, wearing his white lab coat with the worn-out section in the back where he sits most of the day, I'd inhale quickly, glance at the wall clock. He'd have in his hands my graph on which I charted my basal body temperature every morning before doing anything else. He always disapproved of something, grunting before shoving the graph back into the front pocket of the thinning jacket. He'd flip back the paper covers to reveal five, ten, thirty needles, and hold them like darts between the middle and index fingers of his left hand. When he inserted them, I'd feel the heat, sometimes the weight, of the metal breaking through my skin. The one between my eyes always hurt, but not as much as the twenty or so tucked into my lower belly, one by one. And none were as unsettling as the two pins placed on the underside of each breast.

When I first started seeing the acupuncturist, I'd lie awake for the hour between the needles' insertion and their removal, forcing myself to relax, breathe. I'd repeat the names of my fantasy daughters aloud. Jia. Jaehwa. Suyeon. I willed my body to accept his needles. To tolerate his latent sexism, his chiding at my anovulatory cycles, at my age, so that I could feel closer to my ummah. It wasn't just the acupuncture and the old-style medicine. I wanted to give her a grandchild because she had none. Ummah had three children, all in their thirties, and no grandchildren. And I was the eldest. It was my time. So, three times a week I'd lie down on the table, the paper crackling beneath me, and mouth the names of the children I might never have.

Because for the longest time I didn't come from a body, any body, I struggled to imagine anybody coming from mine. Still today, when I think about my biology as either meat or machine, I'm washed over with terror. Never titillated in middle-school health class, always on edge at baby showers, I support public breastfeeding in theory but have to look away because the notion that bodies can give life makes me sick. When conception—our plan B—felt like the only option because I was too critical of how public adoption is practised in Manitoba, I spent a year in therapy trying to ready myself. When the doctors puzzled over why it was taking so long, they ran blood tests and ultrasounds, noted my advanced age, and scolded me for waiting so long. Looked for a physical answer. There was none. I was secretly pleased.

One morning, I gave six vials of blood so that, hopefully, they could figure out why my body was empty. Why my branch was leafless. Fruitless. The little glass tubes toasted each other, tinkling songs that made spritely the panic they held.

I bet they could hear me crying from the waiting room. In fact, I know they could. But I couldn't hold it in, just as I couldn't stop myself from whimpering in languages other than English. I couldn't stop myself from digging my nails into my husband's hand as he witnessed the taking. *Appa*, I moaned, the Korean words for pain and father sounding the same from my mouth. The bilabial *p* burst forth with each quickened breath. I was panting.

It's not really the pain per se. It's the blood. It's the taking of my blood. I used to be okay. But now. I can't stand it.

I'm cold. I'm cold and I'm terrified. I'm cold and I'm terrified and I can only tell that I'm breathing by the way my chest expands and contracts. I don't make a noise. It's nearly five in the morning now. In my mind's eye I can imagine the sky eventually opening up, showing the silhouettes of things that earlier were hidden. I notice I'm not blinking. Then I'm blinking too much. I lick my lip and taste the blood. I lick my lip and feel the deep crack where it's been split apart. On either side of the opening, the skin is starting to get hard and raised up a bit. I chew on it, raking my teeth across the cut until it stops bleeding. There's a single reading lamp in my one-room basement apartment. I kept it on all night long, even before tonight. There is a flimsy lock on the doorknob. The kind they put on bathroom doors in people's homes in Canada. They're not really meant to keep anyone out, but are a hint to possible intruders that maybe they should knock first. I hear the exterior door open and close. It's a glass door, but I can hear it, that's how quiet my breathing is. I count to ten, one number for each breath. I leave my room.

I was partially right. Dawn is not yet here, but at least he is gone. The glass door can be re-locked from inside. What time is it in Montreal? I have no tissues, so I blow my nose on the cold, medicinal face wipes that promo girls stuff into carrier bags each time you buy something in one of the many cosmetics stores in Myeong-dong.

Even if you've just bought a bottle of nail polish, you leave with a bag bursting with freebies. It's uncomfortable to blow your nose into a wet tissue. Actually, in Korea they're literally called water tissues. It feels dirty. I feel dirty. The water tissues make me feel cold.

They come to me, sometimes alone and with secrets whispered only through their eyes. Eyes that tell me everything, because we don't need words to speak the thing we share between us. They come to me in pairs, groups of three or more, bolder, to thank me for telling. And then they're telling, themselves, of the time at the adoptee gathering when girls got together to learn how to paste false eyelashes to monolids and boys plotted separately how to make the most of the situation. When they schemed, *now's our chance*, and took what they knew to be their own fears of never being anyone's first choice and made them weapons aimed at the girls distracted by waterproof mascara. They come to me with stories of that time in Seoul, that adoptee from that place. They ask me if the person who cracked me open was American, which makes me think the person who cracked them open was. We talk softly, between ourselves, older sisters looking out for the younger ones about to go on roots trips alone. We know that in order to find our pasts, our mothers and fathers and anyone else, we spread ourselves out, we open our hearts and bodies and hope for the best.

In 2016, six years after my parents had left in the night, I called my ummah for no other reason than that I was in a Denver hotel and wasn't going to fly back to Canada until the next day at noon. I understood less and less each time we spoke, which at that point hadn't been often, but I tried to listen for the few words I knew. The simple phrases she repeated during each call. But this time she wanted to tell me something important. I couldn't tell if she was saying pain, *I have a lot of pain . . .* or *your father . . .* or even *your father has a lot of pain.* Maybe it didn't matter. The words are too alike, homonyms to my ignorant ear. She started to cry. I think I heard *juk-ah.* To die? dying? dead? She told me to call my sister. I repeated *mul-ah-yo* until she put my father on the phone. We'd not spoken since that night in Montreal. Now he sounded old, too weak to tell me anything more than that he loved me. That and *Appah man-i appa.*

It's funny how quickly we fell back into the old routine of our previous selves, nightly phone conversations with him chiding that I must eat more and me teasing that I wanted to stay thin. Now with the additional promise that I would eat if he would too. He said that he was gaining weight. I didn't believe him, but I let him tell me that anyway. He called me ddal again, with that hard *d* that I can't detect but I know is there because the letter is doubled when written down. Years earlier he thrilled at firing that word, daughter, at me, the possessive and forceful sound at the beginning eventually swallowed and guided by a curved tongue-tip stroking the roof of the mouth. As he was dying, the same word sounded more like a plea.

The colour and shape of the teacups the night my father confirmed that he was dying made me think of the pale-blue eggshells smashed into the sidewalk every May in southern Ontario. I sat at the small IKEA table with my husband to my right and my sister, Bora, to my left. Her husband was next to her. Fourteen hours away, my mother moved into the waiting room to confess that my father was shaving his head as we spoke. I imagined what was left of the thick brown curls he'd passed on to me floating down into the sink, tiny tufts of bunny tails and the mean buzzing of the clippers. She put him on the phone and in English I said, *I don't know what to say.* But he told me he was sorry, that he missed me, loved me, wanted me to come to Korea before it was too late. I felt my husband standing behind me, resting his chin on the top of my head. I saw Bora crying, but I knew it wasn't for him but because she was afraid for our mother. I forgot my fear of flying, my fear of Korea. My fear of my father. I promised to come as soon as I could. He sounded hopeful. His laughter was broken only by his crying and coughing. I imagined him wiping the blood from his lips as these three acts blended together. He laughed again and promised that next year, once he was better, he'd visit me in Canada again. I put a smile into my voice and, with tears falling onto the particleboard tabletop, told him I would pick him up from the airport.

I left Bora's apartment with the news of my father's fate still at the back of my throat where words could not reach. When at last they did, I found myself on the phone with my Canadian parents. I didn't remember dialing.

Unni . . . I listened to a colleague, a friend, discuss her parent's slow fade at the hands of terminal illness. In a few days I'll board a plane and face our own father's nearing death. It won't be gentle; I've learned to expect a hard and painful decline, and if he's lucky, it will be fast. I'll try to remember him by the sound of his voice when he speaks the words I don't understand. I can hear the pebbles in his mouth, the put-on indignation when I call him by his given name, his pouting dissolving into his kingly laugh. But I can't know his mind or his heart.

It was still Winnipeg dark the morning in December 2016 when our luggage was piled into the trunk of the SUV. In the passenger seat, I stared out the window and sipped mineral water as we made our way to the airport. Our husbands chatted to fill the silence, making plans to live together while Bora and I stayed with family in Korea for two weeks. Bora was excited to return but afraid to be apart from her husband for so long; he was trapped in Canada, without documents for the time being. I was afraid to be without my husband too—for other reasons. He'd been with me the first time I made the long journey to Korea, and I didn't know how to arrive in that place, how to anchor myself there, without him.

The trip was long and I was nervous about flying, but I kept myself busy knitting a blanket for my father. The in-flight films were all in English, or dubbed in French, and only a few were about Asian people. That annoyed Bora and me both. We ate the tasteless food and in the last few hours of the journey fixated on the GPS map detailing our route and proximity to Incheon International Airport. We didn't bother trying to sleep.

The reversal happened again the minute we landed. I turned to Bora, needed her, and Bora became protector. The humidity closed around us and I was relieved I was not alone. We laughed that I needed to become more aggressive if I was going to stand a chance against businesswomen in Seoul, who know where they need to go and never hesitate to elbow someone out of the way in order to get there. Bora explained, *you're so careful because you are Canadian. Just keep walking and keep your elbows out*, she advised. *You don't need to learn the formal phrase to apologize for bumping into a stranger. It's never your fault.*

At immigration we were shuffled into separate lines, my sister's taking much longer. In the foreigner line, workers passed out tiny pamphlets from the tourism board and the immigration officer impatiently mimed for me to remove my eyeglasses for the official photograph. An hour later we had our luggage and were in a black taxi heading in the direction of a too-modern airport hotel that smelled like cranberry shampoo. We laughed over the spaghetti dinner we chose, imagining our husbands having a more modest version of the same thing together back in Canada. Then I called our mother, but Bora did all the talking. She requested namul banchan and recommended our mother start cooking immediately for our arrival the next day. Lighthearted because her two girls were back in the country, and we'd come together, Ummah replied, *make it yourself.*

The first night went by quickly, but we were glad we'd resisted Ummah's instructions to take a bus directly to Gimcheon; an extra four hours would have been unimaginable. At the airport hotel, we showered, ate, drank, slept. The hotel seemed empty, tailored to Western sensibilities, with its sleek, almost boutique aesthetic, cloying smell, and cold-cereal breakfast buffet. Hite and Cass were considered imported beers. Even in December, it was humid outside and there was no snow. We were worlds away from the dry, ice-covered winter of our mid-west Canadian home.

At some point in the morning we returned to the airport and bought tickets for a bus that would take us to the small town in the middle of the country. Bora chose soy milk at the station convenience store, while I wanted to remember the taste of cold corn tea. It was dry and hot on the bus, and we coughed throughout the half-day journey. There were small fabric curtains that could awkwardly be closed to block out some of the sunlight, but I wanted to see everything. We were dropped off on the side of the street in front of a grocery store and we worried we were in the wrong place. Abandoned in a small town. A few people milled around, but it was Sunday and the streets were nearly empty. We would come to realize that in Gimcheon many streets are empty every day of the week.

But soon we saw our mother rushing towards us, her gait memorable for its short, shuffling steps. She was wearing a red knit sweater. My father was waiting in the car. Neither Bora nor I expected him to be there. When we reached the old Hyundai that had apparently replaced the Ford sedan from years ago, he got out and lifted the suitcases into the trunk, despite all our protests. He coughed and gasped behind his paper mask. Bora bowed and said something in Korean to which he politely replied. I smiled nervously and looked directly at the only part of his face that was exposed. His eyes welled with tears and he mumbled something I couldn't hear and wouldn't have been able to understand even if I had. We stood like that for a while, forgiving each other.

Skeleton trees on mountains I can see through the cracks in the blinds on the bus to Gimcheon. I have motion sickness. Oksusu tea smells like cold cereal right before I take a sip, but it's more bitter than I remember.

Bora assured me, *you have people. These are your people. They are waiting for you to come. They want you. You don't need to be afraid that you're foreign. This is your mother and this is her home, so this is your home. This is your homecoming. This is the farm where our grandparents grew grapes. You never tasted the grapes from their farm, but they sent a crate every summer and I would eat them so fast I just swallowed the seeds. This is your country too, even if you never get used to the humidity or people get angry that you take too long at the ATM. These are all your people. It's yours too.*

Pear eat, Ummah instructed. Bora corrected her, maybe explaining that, unlike in Korean, word order matters in English. I pointed to her stomach and then the fruit skewered on the tiny white plastic fork with the yellow stains where the tines met, and then I made an undulating motion with my hand and wrist, miming flowing water. *Bae Bae Bae*, I recited, and was rewarded by Ummah's bird-staccato laugh. Homonyms. Stomach, pear, boat. She said I was so smart.

It was the first time I'd seen my mother's home. Here, my parents, nearly thirty years after their first separation, had built their life the way they'd always planned. The restaurant they owned, which they'd closed down temporarily when Appah first fell sick, was a short car ride away. The day we arrived, Ummah cooked a family dinner in her home for her two daughters. She made stew out of some king mushrooms and a block of still-warm fresh tofu. We sat around the folding table set up in the middle of the electric-heated linoleum—made to look like real wood—floor. My father kept one eye on the fish cake soup made without spice just for him and the other on a televised soccer game.

The conversation was hard to follow, but not impossible. Throughout the meal, Bora and I compared the size of different cities, teased our mother about how, in the last week since she'd known we were coming, she'd been too busy gossiping with her friends to take care of the house. On the one hand, it gave Ummah a thrill to describe her daughters as cosmopolitan women, educated and living abroad. On the other, she must have known in her heart she'd lost us both in the end. We were different now. Less hopeful. More cautious.

The fish cake soup was only half eaten when Appah began to choke. He put down his spoon, leaned back against the base of the couch, and turned to the teapot sooner than expected.

In the middle of the night I waited, listening to the rhythm of my father's breathing and the clock on the wall. By two in the morning the gap between the small of my back and the hard floor was making my tailbone ache. Ummah was finally asleep. I slowly un-wove my fingers from hers and left her hand under the quilt. My mother didn't let on that she noticed, and even if she did, she kept her eyes shut as I slipped out and tiptoed back to my private room. A private room in the family home. I wonder if they bought the Western-style bed when they heard I was coming.

My ears narrowed in, focused on the sound of my father's gagging in the next room. How much was he not telling about what was happening in his body in those last months? He hid his naked head and eyebrows with a knit cap pulled down so far it moved each time he blinked. But once, when we entered the house, he was sleeping on the floor and I saw. He quickly reached for his hat and I was ashamed to have been caught seeing him. At dinner he turned away each time his body betrayed him with a gasp or cough that seemed to say, *stop fighting it*. At first the doctors had no hope. Then they said that my father was working hard to take care of himself. Part of that was pretending those hiccups weren't happening, and I got really good at controlling my reaction when they did. At ignoring the noises he made. I barely flinched at all by the end. When I saw my father when the bus dropped us off in Gimcheon, the face mask that was meant to protect him from disease accentuated the wetness of his eyes when I held his face between my hands.

If you walk up a narrow trail just down the street from the place where my mother was raised, you'll pass a modern house with a dog barking in the window. The route is dangerous, not only steep but also filled with bramble and thistles that reach for your arms and legs as you try to keep balance on the rocky trail. It is not worn down enough that the grass is bent, and so it is easy to slip. To the right is a forest that one might imagine sprouted out of sucker branches and other unplanned things. To the left is a quick drop-off. It's important not to look down and to keep up with the others who know the way.

At the top of the incline, the path gives way to a clearing. It's mostly level here. The earth has been moulded into a subtle berm, maybe three-quarters of a foot high and enclosing a patch of about twenty square feet. Inside are two black slabs, staggered, jutting out of grey concrete bases. On each base rests a half-peeled orange, the top section exposed. On one of them there is also a green liquor bottle, partially empty, and a Styrofoam cup containing soju, twigs, and what looks like two drowned flies.

Years ago, on the second occasion with my grandfather, when we'd gathered for Chuseok as family does, he requested soju instead of the traditional breakfast. Now, when I stand before his grave, I wonder if he would like a small cup of the drink on his headstone too. But all there is for him is the rotting fruit, which my mother snatches and flings away. Bora bows deeply two times, and I stand and stare because that's what I've been taught to do. I want to perform the expected Korean customs, but I feel too awkward with everyone watching. I refuse to let myself remember the way I ignored my halabuji the third and final time we saw each other, after I'd mistaken the story and thought he, not my paternal grandfather, had been the person who sent me away. We replace the tossed orange with a half bouquet of purple flowers, saving the other half for the grave under which my eldest uncle lies. This one says he was born in 1957. I struggle to understand the words carved on both of the tombstones. I can't even identify their names. I wonder if my father will be buried here too or somewhere else. I wonder who his people are.

Climbing down the hill takes much more time. The dog is still barking when we get to the bottom, and by now the chickens have also started up. Once there, I look up and see a mass of brown trees, their skeletons tall and narrow. Bare. But one is different. It is leafless, but dotted throughout, like the Christmas bulbs that will soon be carefully unwrapped at home, are bright orange persimmons.

Six women were at a table, but no one was talking. The youngest was thirty, the oldest turned ninety a few months later. The restaurant, which offered a popular style of bibimbap, was empty in comparison with what it's like on weekends, when the line goes out the door. Four of the six had curly heads, which were bent over bowls of rice and seaweed, eggplant and fiery gochujang. Someone gathered food for Halmoni, who ate efficiently, soundlessly. Suddenly the silence was broken when my grandmother looked at me and told me she saw me when I was born. I waited for Bora to translate the words. *You were a pretty baby*, she said twice. So she was there. What did you think, I wondered, when the orphanage worker came to take your first grandchild? Did my prettiness make up for how you have suffered—how you've been blackmailed, how you've been terrorized by fear of exposure?

At some point during my second homecoming, we all moved from Ummah and Appah's house to my aunt's penthouse apartment in nearby Gumi. The first day we were there, I tried to see myself through the eyes of the various people in my various families. To my Korean parents, maybe I was again seen as a celebration. A symbol of a love that had once been denied but was now, decades later, shimmering in the faces of those who tried to have it buried. But to almost everyone else, I was the tripwire that blew shrapnel through at least three generations when I reappeared in 2009. To my older sister, unni, whom I would not see until I was at the airport about to leave Korea for a third time, I embodied years of deception and our father's betrayal. I represented her mother's sadness. For Halmoni, I'd caused years of blackmail, a secret that kept a poor family of grape farmers ground down into the earth. It was impossible not to resent me, with my shining ponytail and designer clothes, even if none of it was my fault and I only dressed this way to make a good impression. To show them respect. Even for Bora, the one to whom I was closest, I had caused pain. Bora's father's rage used to burst open without apparent cause. My sister didn't understand the source of her father's hatred for Ummah. By the time I was revealed to her, she'd long ago stopped speaking to him. My Canadian sister struggled when new Korean siblings were introduced into my life. Sisters with dark hair and black eyes like mine. Sisters. My unni's mother, the slighted woman, was embittered and told to stop coming around the hospital as my father was dying. My halabuji, now buried, had been relieved that the secret was out but resentful of the years wasted running from it. My imo learned that her oldest sister, her closest love, had been hiding what had happened to me for years. My mother eventually got up from the couch and started washing the dishes in her sister's sink when her repeated question to me, *why are you crying?*, went unanswered. My Canadian family took the brunt of my anger and sadness because, unluckily for them, we all spoke the same language. My husband has learned to notice the signs that things are about to split open. He spends his life making sure I have someone to hold on to. I was all of these things, tearing through families and crushing them with my very existence.

If I'm really being honest, the reason I was upset at the hospital wasn't that I was afraid for my father or sad he spent most of the day alone, unable to sleep because of the four other patients sharing the room, including the man who wouldn't stop crying. Well, those aren't the only reasons. I was upset because, when I witnessed his body, I also witnessed my own: now breakable, actually always having been breakable, and out of the shadow of medical enigma. I imagined all of the past doctors' forms I'd filled out with a summary *I'm adopted* scrawled across pages listing various genetic conditions, all those unchecked boxes. Now I know cancer ate my grandfather's stomach, took my mother's uterus, is killing my father, will probably one day end me too. I was upset because, without a past, I used to also be without a future, and in some ways that tore me down but in others it was liberating.

Two calls were made to middle-of-the-night Canada from the same taxi. Two phones rang in separate rooms of the same Winnipeg house. It wasn't clear which call came first, just as it wasn't clear what exact words were spoken because Bora and I, sitting next to each other, knew each other's weak spots and, like sisters, weaponized them. We described the same thing to our helpless but sympathetic husbands, one in Korean, the other in French. Language was a fence we could use to keep each other out. We had privacy even though we were crammed together in the back seat of a sedan. I felt petty, knowing my words would remind my sister that, no matter how hard she studied English, there was always a way to keep her at a distance.

We were coming from the hospital where we'd just left my father and she'd been upset that I started crying when we had to leave him in that place. My mother asked me again and again, *why are you crying?* And I didn't have the words to wonder what she expected me to do in that moment. Her tone felt like an accusation. Ummah was in the front seat of the taxi now. She knew the reason for the calls. She knew her daughters were complaining to their husbands about her, and this knowledge made her look out the window and ignore us.

Ever since they were small, their grandmother had forced all of the cousins to call Bora unni even though she was only a month older than the next-born girl. Bora never cared, but still, she wasn't prepared for the time our eldest cousin came at her, too drunk to even be at a spa. The cousin, the daughter of my eldest, now-dead uncle, lashed out, crying, *I don't want to call you that! I don't even like you!* And Bora was shocked, because she'd never insisted. My sister didn't like it either. But now that I had entered their lives, I've become the oldest of all the cousins, of the entire generation. And that same cousin who felt wronged at having to call Bora by this title even though they were born in the same year doesn't acknowledge me either.

The double bed, pressed against the wall on one side and using the sliding balcony door as a headboard, took up most of the room. There was also a desk with assembled shelves. The kind I had when I was in high school, made of particleboard with wood panelling in back. Two sets of golf clubs leaned against the wall, one set noticeably taller than the other. When I woke up in the middle of the night in imo's apartment, the shorter bag looked like a woman seated at a table, head down in prayer. There was also a vacuum cleaner. The kind used by rich Koreans daily to clean the lapdogs' hair from the large white ceramic floor tiles that heat almost instantly. In the closet, rows of summer polo shirts and linen button-downs hung mismatched from plastic hangers.

It was a perfectly respectable side room. I'm sure that when I was assigned this place to sleep, it was out of fear that my spoiled Western back wouldn't be able to handle the living room floor. And I appreciated the privacy sometimes. But I wanted so much to be a part of my family, even in sleep. Instead, they slept together, Bora, Ummah, and imo, under one blanket. And I was alone with the rest of the storage.

I met my niece. I saw her on video chat because we were still in Gumi, and unni couldn't afford the time off work to leave Seoul even for a few days. I didn't understand much, but I heard my sister tell her daughter that I was her ippun imo, her pretty aunt. She was funny and outspoken, and I had hope for her in the country that never did hold me. She had bangs, just like her mother. She had her eyes. And my hands. The women on that side of my family all have the same hands.

You are my unni's child. Her daughter. We haven't met face to face because I live far from you and I do not even speak Korean! But I saw a photo of you when you were a very small baby and I look at it often. Now I see you streaming on social media. I save every picture and video your ummah shares. When I was a baby, I looked a lot like you. We have the same pouting mouth. Your ummah cuts your bangs like my Canadian mother would cut mine. It's funny, because I always imagined myself a very ugly baby—too round, too brown, eyes too narrow. But you are perfect.

I have no children, but I want them. For many years I didn't want to have babies. I was afraid to think about children coming from inside my body. My Canadian mother used to promise that even though having a baby is painful, in the end the prize was worth it. She meant to be reassuring, but I could only think about the way I'd hurt my own ummah and how she was left prizeless in the end.

Your imo loves you. Not because I know you, but I am certain that if I did, it would only make it more true. I love you because you are my unni's daughter. You are my blood. You are my chance to witness how children can be raised in Korea. No more stories about sorrow and poverty. Stories always show Korea as an unsuitable place to raise children. I'm watching you because you help me unknow that story.

Ummah was both embarrassed and amused when I lightly poked my index finger into the plastic-wrapped rice cake, as if testing the red bean–filled dumpling's hardness. It had been made just a few hours before, so of course it was still soft. Drawn to its pastel stripes, I chose a Styrofoam tray with mujigae-tteok, fluffed up like a crumbling sponge. The cake vendor gave me my change and slipped an extra, individually wrapped piece of cake into my hand as a gift. As we walked away, Ummah remarked that she never gets free gifts when she shops at that stand by herself.

Earlier that week, Ummah peeled and sliced a persimmon, pressed a wedge to my lips, laughed when I swallowed the seed because I didn't know to spit it out. She noticed that I mimicked the way she held her silver chopsticks flat against her palm with her three remaining fingers while manoeuvring her spoon with her thumb and index. Ummah repeated basic words slowly so that I could understand them, repeat them, and hopefully learn them. Just as one does with a toddler venturing into language for the first time. Gam-ja. Potato. My favourite. Every morning, Ummah cut potatoes into matchsticks and fried them with sesame oil and soy sauce.

All of the women were being fitted for rented hanboks in the weeks before my cousin's wedding. His sisters, mother, and aunts, including imo, visited the dressmaker in Gimcheon, who measured their height, the width of their shoulders. Ummah went with them, probably offered uninvited advice. But she didn't allow her eye to linger too long on any one chima. Didn't dare run her fingers through the dip-dyed silk strands of so many norigae, laid-out embellishments that looked deadened when not swinging at the waist, suggestively hinting at what they might be attached to somewhere underneath a woman's jacket. She would not join in the tradition, even though she planned on attending the ceremony. She asked Bora and me to find a wool sweater, something modest, for her to wear instead. As my father lay dying two cities over, my mother would not wear hanbok. She dressed the part of a widow even before that time came.

In Gumi, alone because Bora had a dentist appointment, I returned to the store where we'd bought Christmas decorations the day before. We'd brought the little plastic trees with the white paint dusted on the bristles, meant to look like snow, to the hospital on the morning our mother had to stay home and we were sent to comfort my father by ourselves. The shared hospital room housed three other men that week, and one of them looked on enviously at the attention my father received; later, Appah would share the loaves of bread we'd tucked away in the cupboard.

Again the gift shop in Gumi was filled with teenagers, still in their school uniforms. Hawkish workers followed them around, eyeing their pocketed hands, suspicious of quick movements. Thankfully, no one spoke to me, even though I had mul-ah-yo waiting on my lips. In my mouth. I hastened to the stationery section of the store. I knew exactly where it was. Two weeks in Gumi and we knew the downtown strip by heart. I settled on a set that included five small sheets of notepaper, five matching envelopes, brown with little flowers and leaves printed on one side. At the top of the notepaper, underneath the garland, were the words: *Je vous souhaite du bonheur pour toujours.*

I also found two pens. Black.

The next day, I travelled back to the hospital with Bora while our ummah rested at the apartment. Again we ate at the restaurant across the street and again Appah mostly watched the television screen behind our heads. I felt ashamed that I didn't know, as Bora did, to pour my father a cup of half-hot half-cool water as soon as he sat down. Bora had to ask for an extra cup because I had too quickly filled the ones they had put out with hot tea, thinking I was doing the proper Korean thing. When we left my father at the hospital coffee shop, I handed him some of the notepaper with the French writing on the top. I gave him a black pen. *Please write me a letter,* I asked. Not for the first time. Something inside me needed a record of his handwriting. I suppose I wanted him to do something for me that was difficult.

Two days passed and my father was given a day release from the cancer facility. He drove himself from Daegu to Gumi, about twenty minutes. When he arrived at imo's apartment, where Bora, Ummah, and I had been staying, he sat in the middle of the sectional couch and locked his eyes on the television. He wore the same workout pants and knit sweater he'd had on when he was admitted. He wore a baseball cap and a paper mask over his face. He ate, without looking away from the screen, the potato pancakes and Chinese-style tofu I'd prepared for him earlier that morning.

I wanted my father to look at me, but he seemed happy just to have me next to him while he flipped through the channels as if it was any old day. Right before he was scheduled to leave, to drive himself back to the hospital, I asked for my letter. He said something I didn't understand, but I quickly recognized from his tone that he hadn't written it. The habitual resentment started to rise up again. The selfishness I'd tried to ignore because of the cancer made my lip twitch, my eyes narrow. My father looked away. He made me promise to return in the summer. I said I would. I told him I loved him, but my mouth was filled with acid. That would be the last time my father and I were together.

Inside the purple suitcase with the yellow Hudson's Bay Company bag tied around its handle like a ribbon were two weeks of clothes, ten kilos of juice (grape, apple, and pear housed in half-cup bags), air-dried radishes for tea, and enough gochugaru flakes to last three years. Ummah sat on the ceramic floor with Bora and me, preparing food for the ten-hour journey across the Pacific Ocean with the hope that customs workers would find no reason to search. I was not afraid that I'd be bringing across any forbidden items, it was just that it was the first time I'd undertaken this effort. That night, when we sat with our mother on the floor, packing the luggage together, for the first time I felt like an immigrant to Canada. I liked it.

Ni-How, they said before ruptured laughter. *Ni-How-Ma?*
It was dark and Bora and I were walking arm in arm,
trying to find the path from the metro station to our
hotel room in Seoul. There was a distant ruckus from a
bar a few blocks off, but otherwise no one was around.
The neighbourhood was empty. And it was quiet. Every
shop on the street was a furniture store closed for the
night. Rows of identical chairs and tables, some turned
upside down with their spindly legs jutting into the air.
We crossed the street to get away from the two drunk
men who'd mistaken us for tourists. Bora thought little
of it, but I was sad that even in Korea, now with my hair
its natural dark colour, men on the street *Ni-How*ed me.
They'd obviously registered that we weren't speaking
Korean, that I couldn't speak Korean, and this was
enough to make me foreign again. I explained this to
Bora, who realized at last that the white Canadian men
who'd been shouting this to her on the street in
Winnipeg were trying to get her attention, and that they
were doing it in presumptuous ways. *But I'm not even
Chinese*, Bora laughed incredulously.

Unni . . . The last time I saw you, Bora and I were on our way back to Canada and it was so busy at ICN that day you were only able to slip away for ten minutes. At a vacant gate in the international terminal, I was the middle sister. The only link between Bora and you. Half of me with you, half with her. It was the only time the three of us would be together. I could feel the tightness between you and me, unni, as though we dreaded what was to happen. Not our father's death, but the slow wake that would stream out from it when the time finally came. Like the crest that vees out from the stern of a boat as it sails through the water, we'd be gently but irrevocably ushered apart.

Back in Winnipeg, by the time I learned that my father's cancer had spread from his lungs to his brain, everyone else had been talking about it for weeks. They kept things from me because they thought they were protecting me, as if they believed I was too fragile to know truths about them.

The second bus that my sister rides on her way to class in the far outskirts of Winnipeg is always empty around two in the afternoon. It passes the suburbs. It passes the big-box-store shopping centres, and the 1960s subdivisions built so that white families wouldn't have to mix with the brown and Black people edging dangerously close to their neighbourhoods of two-storey houses and regal elm trees. No one speaks to her, but whenever enough people are on board that strangers need to sit side by side, she's always the first person to be chosen as a partner. She looks out the window, seeing the faint outline of her reflection mirrored back. Her straight black eyelashes. Her thin hair in need of cutting. Bora's bag is stuffed with the two-hundred-dollar textbook that came with the tuition fees she paid to the vocational school that still refuses to release her health card for some bureaucratic reason neither of us understands. Her bag also holds her uniform, because today she has to intern at the college cafeteria. Her ponytail will form a perfect loop when it's constrained by the black hairnet that otherwise disappears on her.

It's June, and six months since we travelled to Korea to visit my dying father. Six months, and finally I've admitted that I cannot read the letter our mother wrote to me on that last night before we left Gumi for Seoul. Where my father had ignored my request, my mother not only accepted but wrote a letter to Bora too. I tried, stubbornly, many times to understand it on my own. The letter on the notepaper with the French words, penned in black ink. So, commuting to her campus south of the city, my sister reads the letter meant only for me from our mother.

My dearest daughter, Heijun.

Can you imagine the sadness that has been in my heart throughout my whole life? It is mostly you that is the sadness in my heart. There are times when I don't want to think about you and so I forget you for long periods. I cannot bring myself to imagine you growing up with a different mother. I felt so ashamed for what I had done to you. What I let happen to you.

But because of you, I met your father again, and he gives me so much love. Even though bad things happened in the past, now I am happy. I was happy. However, your father is sick and it's making this so difficult again. I thought about it for a long time before telling you. I wasn't sure if you would care. I didn't know what you would say. It had been so many years since we left you in Montreal. How many times can you forgive your mother for leaving you in the night?

Thank you for coming from Canada. It is so far, too far, from Korea. Thank you for forgiving us.

My loving daughter, Heijun. I never thought that I would meet you. I'd resigned myself to never meeting you for the rest of my life. But then we met and your father and I are finally happy. I hope that we can meet again often.

Thank you for being so kind to your younger sister. I hope you and Bora will get along and love each other like you do now. I hope that never changes.

I'm sorry. You came all the way from Canada and I didn't really take care of you. I don't know how to take care of you. I think I never did. I'm sorry. But I will try to remain positive and cheerful and I hope that you will come back to Korea to visit your father and me.

I love you. My daughter.

It took months for it to slowly draw to its end. He died in the morning—but for me, fourteen hours back in time, it was the night before. I got up from the table, my phone still in my hand. I learned my father's death by text message. I looked down and I'd wrapped a scarf around my throat. My boots were suddenly on.

It was December again. I walked out into the dark night. It was snowing. It fluttered down like woolly pollen. I walked for hours in the snow. And that was it.

Months after, I was flying to Vancouver. I awoke mid-flight with the realization that my father was dead and that I'd never see him again. Outside, an ocean of clouds was spread thick forever and ever.

Unni . . . I saw our father at home via video chat the week before he died. His bald head had many black marks on it. I looked away, but wondered if they'd always been there or if they were a product of his aggressive drug regimen. He quickly put on a cap, chastising my mother for showing him without it. I asked him if he was in pain. He said no. When he saw me on the screen, his eyes filled with tears.

Unni, thank you for trying to explain things to me. I know you have your own child to take care of. Thank you for taking care of me too, using words that were probably hard to find. I know my vocabulary is more limited than your daughter's, but my questions are those of a grown woman.

What were our father's last words, unni? What was the last thing he said to you? I tried to remember the sounds he made after I promised to call again soon. I hold on to those noises, but I know they will soon leave my memory. Words without language fall away too easily. Did you forgive him as he was dying, unni? Should I forgive him as well?

My Canadian mother asked me one night, *where do you want to be buried?* She meant, do I want to be buried in Korea? Sent back after all this time? When she asked me that, I realized that my body doesn't belong to any place. And it doesn't belong *in* any place.

Soon after Appah died, a new year began. In late afternoon on the first day of 2018, I swore at the many small bowls placed inside the deep soup dishes as I struggled to find the large-enough one in time. I imagined the noodles melting into slop. The shrill oven timer added to my panic. A housecoat covered flannel pants and the cotton dress I had worn the day before and then through the night. My wet hair was in a towel. It was so long that the ends peeked out and dripped a line of cold water down the centre of my back. Two massive glass jars sat on the countertop. One contained what was left of the chili flakes my mother double-bagged and packed in my luggage. In the other were the dried radishes that only my husband used to make tea. I chose two mismatched wooden chopsticks from the drawer, noting that the skinny end of one was warped, but it didn't matter. I was anxious to eat Korea, and I slammed the food into my mouth even though it was so hot it hurt.

One night my husband's friends joined us for a last-minute dinner at our house. And midway through my preparations I realized the significance of the kimchi stew and potato noodles I was making. The habitual food that my hands now knew without thinking was the food I'd learned to eat and cook and love as a grown woman. And that felt very real.

Because there is no Korea for me without her, and by that I mean I could not return unless I knew I had people there who wanted me, I find it hard to imagine going back ever again if Ummah dies. If she dies before me. And it's more than all that. How could I ever go back if she's no longer there? When every memory of that place is her? Korea is nothing without my mother.

I've learned from Bora that Korean children call their parents on their own birthday. It's different from what happens in Canada, where the person celebrating is on the receiving end of cards and phone calls and visits. It changed everything this year, because it meant I didn't have to wait for Ummah to find me. To prove that she was thinking of me on that one day. And when I found her, and she shouted my name, rejoiced and asked me if I was happy, I let my heart uncurl and the fear spilled through to my fingertips, gravel onto the ground.

I needed to distill my heart. Sometimes I loved so hard it hurt. It hurt me and it hurt them. But I didn't know how to stop.

By the time 2018 revealed itself, my heart was tired. Ten years had passed between the day I started the reunion with my Korean family and the moment when I learned to accept the grief that would always live there.

When a new life arrived in our home, it both was and wasn't a surprise. We'd completed home studies years earlier, before even considering conception ourselves. The training courses we took never imagined someone like me in the room. Darker, more cautious, more alert to the narratives being told than the average applicant. More than once I sank into myself when applicants were cajoled with the assurance that, even with open access, they could control how often children would see their parents. When social workers promised that parental interest usually drops off after a certain point. Five years or so after the completion of the courses, a worker asked if we'd loosen our restrictions on race. I refused. They asked if we'd consider another country. Something closed. Something private. But I'm not the kind of woman who wanted to become that kind of mother in that kind of way. That's when I started to entertain the emotional possibility of conception. I went to a fertility clinic. And an acupuncturist. I saw a therapist.

But then she arrived.

When she came to live with us, I told my mother with the only word I had and that she'd understand, imprecise and imperfect as it was. *Ddal*. Ummah appeared nervous and I assumed she spoke with Bora later that night. The morning after the announcement, Ummah sent two text messages. To me, they were unclear. My sister later translated. Roughly:

1. I hope that you will be a good mother.
2. I'm sorry. I couldn't show you how.

Unni . . . At one month, already her hair was so black and her eyes were so black too. You won't see our father, yourself, or even me in her perfect face. But you must have known that none of that would ever matter. I told you once that, upon seeing my mother's picture for the first time, my heart cracked open and I thought I might die. Ten years and so much life passed between seeing that photograph of Ummah and the one that now hangs on my refrigerator door next to tiny handprints inked on card stock and coupons for DHA-enriched formula. I saw her too for the first time through a photograph.

Unni. I run the pads of my thumbs over the soft fronds of her eyelashes and she stares back, never blinking. My baby finger fits perfectly into the arch of her small mouth. She smells sweet, so I crave sugar all the time. Is that normal? Once, she gazed into my eyes as she was drifting away. She didn't fight sleep, like sometimes she does. She just lowered her eyes and we lay face to face, one breath between us, until she woke, unsurprised to see me watching her still.

When your daughter was born, did you brush your lips against the down circling at the crown of her head? Did you tuck her into a podaegi so you could sense her heart beating between your shoulder blades? Did you press her ear to the hollow of your throat so she could feel the tremble of your voice as you sang her to sleep? Did you buy her a white dress and a white cake made of rice flour to celebrate her hundredth day? Tell me. Unni . . . Am I doing it right?

They caution. They say nothing is for certain. They say love her with your head but be careful with your heart. They say hold her in your arms but know that there are forces stronger than a mother's embrace. And although I know better than to trust systems, to trust kinship, I place in her small hands my whole life.

Dearest one,

When first you came into my life, only six months after my father—your halabuji—died, everyone laughed and asked if I was sleeping. It was not your crying that kept me awake all night. I stayed up listening to you breathe. Listening to your heart. Lullabies catching in my throat.

I traced the stars on your ceiling with my fingertip from down there, my back on the nursery floor. I could not bring myself to be away. All night I watched over you, knowing it was daytime in Korea. I'd wipe my tears away with the cold towelettes that we kept in a box on your changing table. They felt cold. They opened my eyes.

My love. You break my heart into a thousand pieces in a way I've never before known. You devastate me with your smallness. I hold the palm of my hand to your body as you sleep. I feel your chest rise and fall with your dreams. Your heart is a moth with wings fluttering against my fingertips. I sleep on the unheated wood floor next to your crib so I can reach between the slats and you'll know, always, I am here.

A Korean proverb. 딸은 엄마 팔자를 따라간다.
The daughter follows the path of her mother.

Acknowledgements

There are too many people to thank in such a small space. Please forgive me for my brevity and insufficiency as well as for any inevitable absences here.

This memoir was written around the world, but mostly in Treaty 1 Winnipeg, Manitoba, on the traditional lands of the Anishinaabeg, Cree, Oji-Cree, Dakota, and Dene People, and the homeland of the Métis nation; in Palo Alto, California, on the traditional lands of the Ohlone Peoples; and at the Banff Centre for Art and Creativity, on the traditional lands of the Stoney Nakoda, Blackfoot, and Tsuut'ina Peoples. As a guest in all of these places, I offer my most genuine and committed appreciation. Thank you.

I'd like to offer my gratitude also to the owners of, and volunteers at, the Korean adoptee guesthouse in Seoul. Thank you for your work and thank you for many of the things you offer.

Martha Kanya-Forstner. I trust your editorial brilliance with all my heart. I've said it throughout this journey. You are a genius. Thank you for your gentle but direct guidance. Thank you for your vision for this book and your faith that I could ever live up to what you somehow see in me. Even in the most difficult times, I know your heart was with me.

Thank you to Terri Nimmo for the gorgeous work you produced in the design of this book. You imagine and then create such beauty. Thank you, John Sweet, for your careful help and guidance. Allie McHugh—thank you for your dedication to this project and all round excellence. I'm so happy it's you. Erin Kelly and team—thank you for helping me in all the ways you have. I'm in awe. Thank you to Joe Lee for your keen eye, kind support, and feeling of community. You must know how it is especially meaningful that you've been an integral part of this book.

Jackie Kaiser. You are so smart, so dedicated, so generous. I'm amazed by my fortune at having you as my agent and ally and friend. Thank you for holding me together. I really cannot thank you and your colleagues at Westwood Creative Artists enough. I'm humbled.

David Chariandy. Carrianne Leung. Hiromi Goto. Joshua Whitehead. Lee Herrick. Jennifer Kwon Dobbs. Viet Thanh Nguyen. Junot Diaz. Canisia Lubrin. Alicia Elliott. Alexander Chee. Whitney French. Minelle Mahtani. Cason Sharpe. Devyani Saltzman. Susan Ito. You've offered guidance and support in many areas and in many ways. Thank you for bringing light and beauty, love and laughter into the world. Into my world. Thank you for your courage.

Gwen Benaway. Natalie Wee. Prathna Lor. Rebecca Salazar Leon. Dallas Hunt. Nickita Longman. Larissa Lai.

Délice Mugabo. Alexa Potashnik. David Palumbo-Liu. Chim Undi. Eleanor Ty. Lily Cho. Lee So Hee. Les Sabiston. Karrie-Noelle Plohman. Catherine Hunter. Jane Barter. Angela Failler. Owen Toews. David Churchill. Bronwyn Dobchuk-Land. Roewan Crowe. Kristin Fillingham. Brandon Christopher. Readers, listeners, supporters, all. You inspire me in more ways than you might ever know.

Aviaq Risager. Kimberly McKee. Amandine Gay. Indigo Willing. Tobias Hübinette. Nate Kupel. Daniel Drennan ElAwar. David Warburton. Kit Myers. Emily Bartz. Kim Park Nelson. Susan Devan Harness. Annaka van Huizen. Felicity Elsted. Joseph Pierce. Mariama J. Lockington. Bert Ballard. Thank you for seeing me and allowing me to see you.

My brilliant BIPOC students and colleagues at the University of Winnipeg. Thank you for ongoing lessons on how to live with dignity and integrity and love. Thank you to the Banff Centre and everyone involved in the *Centering Ourselves* writing residency. Thank you to my colleagues and friends at The Alliance for the Study of Adoption and Culture.

At the very last moment in this book's production, the world again collapsed around me. Around us. A community of people showed another kind of kinship and it is so valuable. I'm heartbroken. But I'm also uplifted by your love. Thank you. This book is also for you.

Many families. It is difficult. Thank you for your patience and trust. Thank you for your love in the many ways it can be given and received. Thank you for your forgiveness. Thank you for always being. Thank you for coming when I needed you most. Thank you for trying to hold me in one piece. I love you.

My Friend. You are so much more than who I'd dreamed you to be. When one of the most devastating things that could happen to a person happened to me, you came to me. You helped me finish this book and tried to plant hope in me for a future I'm still not certain I can see. I love you.

My Sister. I would live this life again and again if it meant each time you were there, at the end, standing next to me. This has always been about you. You must know that. I love you.

My Husband. There is no me without you. There is nothing at all without you. Please hold on to me forever as I will you. You're not alone. I love you.

Baby. Thank you. I love you. I always will.